WARRIOR • 149

AFRIKAKORPS SOLDIER 1941–43

PIER PAOLO BATTISTELLI   ILLUSTRATED BY RAFFAELE RUGGERI

Series editor Marcus Cowper

First published in Great Britain in 2010 by Osprey Publishing
Midland House, West Way, Botley, Oxford OX2 0PH, UK
44-02 23rd St, Suite 219, Long Island City, NY 11101, USA
E-mail: info@ospreypublishing.com

A CIP catalogue record for this book is available from the British Library.

ISBN: 978 1 84603 688 0
E-book ISBN: 978 1 84908 298 3

Editorial by Ilios Publishing Ltd, Oxford, UK (www.iliospublishing.com)
Cartography Map Studio, Romsey, UK
Page layout by Mark Holt
Index by Sandra Shotter
Typeset in Sabon and Myriad Pro
Originated by PPS Grasmere, Leeds, UK
Printed in China through Worldprint Ltd

10 11 12 13 14 10 9 8 7 6 5 4 3 2 1

AUTHOR ACKNOWLEDGEMENTS

The author would like to thank for their help his friends and colleagues (in no particular order): Prof Piero Crociani, Dr Christopher Pugsley, Dr Klaus Schmider, Dr Andrea Molinari, Dr Angelo Luigi Pirocchi, Dr Federico Peyrani and Mr Carlo Pecchi.

ARTIST'S NOTE

Readers may care to note that the original paintings from which the colour plates in this book were prepared are available for private sale. All reproduction copyright whatsoever is retained by the Publishers. All enquiries should be addressed to:

Raffaele Ruggeri,
Via Indipendenza 22,
Bologna, 40121,
Italy

The Publishers regret that they can enter into no correspondence upon this matter.

THE WOODLAND TRUST

Osprey Publishing are supporting the Woodland Trust, the UK's leading woodland conservation charity, by funding the dedication of trees.

FOR A CATALOGUE OF ALL BOOKS PUBLISHED BY OSPREY MILITARY AND AVIATION PLEASE CONTACT:

Osprey Direct, c/o Random House Distribution Center,
400 Hahn Road, Westminster, MD 21157
Email: uscustomerservice@ospreypublishing.com

Osprey Direct, The Book Service Ltd, Distribution Centre,
Colchester Road, Frating Green, Colchester, Essex, CO7 7DW
E-mail: customerservice@ospreypublishing.com

www.ospreypublishing.com

CONTENTS

AFRIKAKORPS SOLDIER 1941–43

THE AFRIKAKORPS

The origins of the Deutsches Afrikakorps date back to October 1940, when Hitler offered Mussolini a German Panzer division for North Africa. For this purpose 3. Panzer-Division was chosen, but it was neither trained nor equipped for the arid climate. Mussolini's ill-fated venture against Greece, started at the end of that month, saw the proposal stall at first and early in December as the situation worsened in the Mediterranean it was cancelled by Hitler himself. General O'Connor's counter-attack against the Italian positions at Sidi Barrani turned into a full offensive, which, by early February 1941, threatened to drive the Italians out of Libya. On 9 January, facing the new situation, Hitler had decided that the Italians had to be helped and ordered the creation of 'blocking detachment Libya' (Sperrverband Libyen) to help prevent any further British advance. Formed from elements of the 3. Panzer-Division, it became leichte-Division Funck (named after its commander) on 14 January, soon redesignated 5. leichte-Division. By 14 February 1941 its first elements, namely the reconnaissance and the anti-tank detachments (Aufklärungs-Abteilung 3 and Panzerjäger-Abteilung 39) had arrived in Tripoli, and four

Two officers in discussion over a map. The man on the right is a Knight's Cross recipient. The board was probably put there to name a place after someone, the word *Ras* meaning either a peak or being used to mark the point were a wadi begins. (HITM)

days later Hitler gave the order to bring the German forces in North Africa up to strength by sending another Panzer division (the 15. Panzer-Division) and by creating the headquarters of the 'Deutsches Afrikakorps', which was put under the command of General Erwin Rommel (who had already arrived in Tripoli on 12 February).

The actual state of the German unpreparedness for the war in the Western Desert is hard to fathom; uniforms were the only desert item actually available, and vehicles arrived in Libya still painted in the European standard dark grey. Rommel, albeit a successful Panzer division commander during the campaign against France, had no experience as a corps commander or of the desert. Units were mostly equipped for the European theatre, and would soon prove unsuitable for North Africa, not to mention the absolute lack of any kind of acclimatization to an unfamiliar and harsh environment. Yet, thanks both to Rommel's initiative and to the British diversion in Greece (where an attempt was made to prevent the country being defeated by the Germans), the Afrikakorps was on the move as early as 31 March 1941 and leading elements seized the Mersa Brega position. Agedabia followed on 2 April, marking the beginning of Afrikakorps' first offensive into Cyrenaica, an offensive that halted ten days later at the Egyptian border without claiming its most precious objective, Tobruk, which was firmly held by Australian troops. This first offensive gave both the Afrikakorps and its commander widespread notoriety and successfully established the ground for future myths, yet it could not cover up the weaknesses of the German forces in North Africa. Rommel's mistakes apart, men of the Afrikakorps lacked both adequate training and experience to face their enemies on equal terms, and were absolutely unfit to attack a well-established and defended position like the Tobruk perimeter.

An SdKfz 251 troop transport medium half-track, probably belonging to a unit's headquarters as denoted by the pennant. Note how the frontal machine gun is heavily wrapped to prevent sand getting into it. (HITM)

Mechanized warfare in the desert: an Afrikakorps column moves at full speed along a track. The column includes light Kübelwagen staff cars, medium Opel Blitz lorries and SdKfz 10 prime movers, which are half-tracks towing 50mm Pak 38 anti-tank guns. (HITM)

Supply problems surfaced and the Afrikakorps was stalled for months, unable to seek any solution other than merely wait for new units to arrive, store supplies and wait for the right moment to storm the Tobruk defences.

By May 1941 the Afrikakorps was already taking shape, and the successes against the British attacks that stormed the Sollum position on the Egyptian border in May (Operation *Brevity*) and June (Operation *Battleaxe*) suggested it was already the efficient fighting force that might achieve at its true strategic goal of reaching the Suez Canal. However, it was not ready yet. Some order was instilled over the organizational chaos during the summer, with the creation of the headquarters of Panzergruppe Afrika under Rommel's command on 15 July (actually formed one month later) and with a major reorganization of units, which took place on 1 August. The 5. leichte-Division became the 21. Panzer-Division, subordinate units were shuffled and, following an order of 26 June, the headquarters of the 'Afrika Division' (since 28 November 1941

General Ludwig Crüwell (left) along with an Afrikakorps staff officer who is also a Knight's Cross recipient. Crüwell took over command of the Afrikakorps from Rommel on 15 August 1941 and on 1 September was awarded oak leaves to his Knight's Cross. He was captured on 29 May 1942 during the battle of Gazala, when his Storch aircraft was shot down. (HITM)

known as the 90. leichte-Afrika-Division) was created, even though the division started forming near Tobruk only in late October. The battle of Operation *Crusader* on 18 November 1941 (known to the Germans as *Winterschlacht* or 'winter battle') is a good example of the Afrikakorps' strengths and weaknesses. It could win the day like it did in on 23 November at the battle of *Totensonntag* ('Sunday of the dead'), but it did so at a very high price. Rommel's decision to launch his 'dash to the wire' eventually provided the British forces with the chance to relieve the besieged Tobruk garrison. When, following see-saw clashes at Sidi Rezegh between 30 November and 2 December, Rommel eventually ordered withdrawal first to the Gazala Line and then to Agedabia on 5–6 December, the Afrikakorps was a beaten but not defeated force. Lack of supplies and reinforcements once more influenced this decision, and it is worth noting that Rommel's second drive into Cyrenaica took place shortly after the arrival, on 5 January 1942, of a supply and reinforcement convoy at Tripoli.

The second drive started on 21 January and ended, after much success, on 6 February 1942 with the Afrikakorps facing the Gazala Line. For the months to come the Afrikakorps took advantage of the lull period to rest, refit and reorganize once more. When the attack against the Gazala Line was unleashed on 26 May 1942, the Afrikakorps was undoubtedly at its best. The battle that followed was neither easy nor straightforward; in two days Rommel's plan was thwarted, and between late May and early June the Afrikakorps fought with its back to the enemy's wire and minefields, repulsing British counter-attacks and conquering their strongholds on the line. It might well have turned into defeat but, this time, German superiority was remarkable. Once free to fight in the open, the Afrikakorps took full advantage of its skills and capabilities and inflicted serious losses to the enemy, first on 11–13 June at El Adem and then on 14–15 June at the battle of El Acroma. Eventually, on 20–21 June, Tobruk was stormed and seized with minimal losses on the German side and heavy losses for the British. The Afrikakorps' final goal, the Suez Canal, was in sight.

Rommel, promptly promoted to the rank of *Generalfeldmarschall*, wasted no time in trying to grasp a unique opportunity; as early as 22 June he set the Afrikakorps in motion toward the Egyptian border, which was crossed on

Infantry had a role to play in the Western Desert as well as armour. Here a platoon, including a machine-gun section (left), moves past a burning vehicle. Note how some are wearing the overcoat while others just their uniform jackets. (HITM)

23–24 June. Two days later the Afrikakorps was at Mersa Matruh, which was itself stormed and seized on 27–28 June while the British forces withdrew to their last defence line before the Nile at El Alamein. The first battle for Alamein started on 1 July, but it was soon clear that Rommel had driven his Afrikakorps beyond all limits; losses and exhaustion caused by attrition took their toll, and the Australian counter-attack on 10–11 July brought the first real crisis upon the German forces. Even though the first battle for Alamein lasted until 27 July, the illusion of reaching the Suez Canal had melted away. In August reinforcements were brought in, including Fallschirmjäger-Brigade Ramcke and the 164. leichte-Division, altering the balance within the Afrikakorps so that it was now made up more of infantry than of armoured units. The last attempt to break through the Alamein line at the battle of Alam Halfa, which lasted from 30 August to 6 September 1942, soon ran short of strength because of the British defence and from a lack of supplies. In the weeks that followed, the Afrikakorps could do little but prepare to face the enemy onslaught in a kind of war it was not prepared for, and for which it was completely unfit to fight.

When the Alamein battle started on 23 October 1942 little was left of the original Afrikakorps. Nevertheless, the Germans fought with determination until, on 4 November, Rommel ordered the retreat. Four days later the Allied landing in French North Africa opened a new front, and in a matter of days the Germans established a bridgehead in Tunisia. By then the Afrikakorps had withdrawn to the Egyptian border at Sollum, which was no longer a defensible position. The last retreat was a skilled one, even though every Afrikakorps soldier knew that it was a one-way road. After holding out for a while at Mersa Brega (from 24 November to 12 December) the march back started again and on 22 January 1943 Tripoli was evacuated. A few days later the Afrikakorps started to move into Tunisia, where a defence line was set up by mid-February 1943; this was to be the last chapter in the history of the Afrikakorps.

CHRONOLOGY

1940

10 June	Italy enters World War II.
October	General Thoma is sent to Libya in advance of the planned sending of the 3. Panzer-Division to North Africa.
4 December	Hitler announces the planned sending of German troops to North Africa.

1941

9 January	Hitler declares his intention to send a 'blocking formation' (*Sperrverband*) to Libya to help the Italians.
3 February	Erwin Rommel is appointed Commander-in-Chief of the German Army troops in Libya.
12 February	Rommel arrives in Tripoli.

14 February	The first units of 5. leichte-Division arrive at Tripoli; the entire division is transported to North Africa by early April.
18 February	Hitler orders the creation of a German corps headquarters for North Africa.
26 February	The 15. Panzer-Division is selected as the second German division for North Africa.
24 March	First clash between German and British forces near El Agheila.
10–14 April	Tobruk is surrounded; the first attacks by elements of the 5. leichte-Division are repulsed.
30 April to 4 May	A second German attack against the Tobruk perimeter (the battle of Ras el Mdauuar) fails.
15–17 June	British launch Operation *Battleaxe* against Sollum and Bardia; they are repulsed with heavy losses.
15 July	Orders are issued for the creation of the headquarters of Panzergruppe Afrika under Rommel's command.
1 August	The 5. leichte-Division is renamed the 21. Panzer-Division.
15 August	Rommel takes command of Panzergruppe Afrika.
18 November	British Eighth Army launches Operation *Crusader*, with the aim of relieving the Tobruk garrison.
5–6 December	Rommel orders withdrawal to the Gazala Line.

1942

22 January	Panzergruppe Afrika is renamed Panzerarmee Afrika.
11–13 June	Battle of El Adem, where the Afrikakorps inflicts heavy losses on the British armoured forces.
20–21 June	Tobruk is stormed and seized.
22 June	The Afrikakorps crosses the Egyptian border in its pursuit eastwards.
1–3 Jul	First German attacks against the Alamein Line; they fail to achieve a breakthrough.
30 August to 6 September	Rommel's second attack against the Alamein Line, with a flanking movement that is halted at the Alam Halfa ridge; lacking supplies and facing overwhelming British superiority, the Afrikakorps withdraws to its starting positions.

2–4 November	The decisive days of the battle of El Alamein; Eighth Army achieves a breakthrough that the Germans cannot contain or counter-attack; Rommel orders retreat westwards.
8 November	Allied forces land in French North Africa as part of Operation *Torch*.

1943

22 January	Tripoli is evacuated, and seized by Eighth Army the following day; start of Afrikakorps' final retreat into Tunisia.
23 February	Rommel takes command of the newly formed Heeresgruppe Afrika.
9 March	Rommel leaves North Africa and is replaced at the head of Heeresgruppe Afrika by General Jürgen von Arnim.
19 April	Last Allied offensive in North Africa begins.
13 May	Axis forces in North Africa surrender, and the Afrikakorps ceases to exist.

RECRUITMENT AND ENLISTMENT

Early in 1941 the German Panzer divisions were at their peak, with a large number of trained and experienced personnel available, a condition that would dramatically change some months later and which would not be experienced again during the rest of the war. Since 1935, national service in Germany had seen men being selected at the age of 18–19, and if fit for active duty serving until they were 22. After that they were put in the reserve, which was divided into three different categories: fully available for recall, limited availability for recall and the Ersatz Reserve (replacement reserve), which had an even more limited availability for recall. Older soldiers, those aged between 35 and 45, were part of the Landwehr, and those between 45 and 55 were part of the Landsturm. At the end of 1940 all the Panzer and motorized infantry divisions were made up of youngsters aged between 23 and 25, serving mainly in front-line units. Support units and technical services were mostly composed of soldiers aged between 32 and 35, and a good deal of them possessed combat experience gained during the campaigns against Poland in 1939 and France in 1940.

Both the 5. leichte-Division (later renamed as the 21. Panzer-Division) and the 15. Panzer-Division enjoyed such advantages in the matter of personnel, which certainly contributed to their early successes. However, the selection of personnel had not taken into account the needs and requirements of service in desert areas. When orders for transfer to Libya were issued, the medical orderly of the 15. Panzer-Division's reconnaissance detachment (Panzer-Aufklärungs-Abteilung 33) tested his men in a very simple way: each one was to swallow eight quinine tablets, and whoever failed to do so was marked unfit for desert duty. Also, some companies had a kind of intelligence test that asked men to point out the difference between the word *Kiste* and the rarer

Officers of the 15. Panzer-Division check a map in the field. The officer in the white shirt (privately purchased) pointing at the map has the insignia of Aufklärungs-Abteilung 33 on his European peaked cap, between the eagle and the cockade. (HITM)

Kasten (both meaning box, chest or crate). Not all those marked unfit for desert duty were actually expelled from the unit, and some of them would perform well in North Africa in spite of their lack of fitness. Replacements for the rejected men came from the replacement units, which were also intended to provide replacements later on during the campaign.

In the German Army every unit was raised locally, with people coming from a specific area. This had the clear purpose of strengthening ties amongst servicemen and of making units homogenous. The basic recruitment area was the *Wehrkreis* (military district), where units were raised either locally in a given town or county, or thoroughout the district. The former was mostly the case for infantry and other large units, whilst the latter was for all-volunteer units like the Panzer regiments or some other technical units. Following mobilization, every unit had a 'twin' left at its home barracks; this was made up of a cadre filled either with new intakes or with those wounded who, after being sent back home for treatment and recovery, eventually rejoined their home unit. As an example, the 15. Panzer-Division's Schützen-Regiment 104, based in Landau in Wehrkreis XII, drew its replacements from Schützen-Ersatz-Bataillon 104, which could replace either individual soldiers (as in the case of those unfit for desert duties) or, at the completion of basic training, create replacement companies of 200 men. These could be put together to form 'march battalions' of 1,000 men that would be sent to join their parent unit at the front.

A major reorganization of the replacement system for the Afrikakorps was started in June 1942. There were minor changes to recruitment areas, which for example had the 15. Panzer-Division's reconnaissance detachment being moved from Wehrkreis XII to III and its communication unit moved from Wehrkreis V to XI. Also, and more importantly, in July new regulations were introduced further tightening (on paper at least) the selection process. From then on all replacements for Afrikakorps units had to be fit for service in desert

The headquarters of a tank battalion from the 15. Panzer-Division's Panzer-Regiment 8 in 1941, including a command PzKpfw III Ausf. H (sporting the letter 'I' on the turret and the divisional insignia on the left hull) and an SdKfz 251/1 half-track. (HITM)

areas. The focus was on age, with the exception of those who volunteered for service in North Africa. Replacements for both combat and support units had to be chosen from those born in the years 1914–1922, which corresponded to those aged between 20 and 28. It did not take long before problems started to surface, given both the heavy casualty rate suffered during the battles on the Gazala Line and the advance into Egypt (especially in front-line combat units) and the concurrent ever-growing need for replacements for the Eastern Front. In August the figures were quite unbalanced, with losses far exceeding replacements; thus, even though it was during this month that Afrikakorps strength reached its peak of 57,000 men, mostly thanks to the arrival of new units, its divisions were short of 480 officers, 2,500 NCOs and 9,000 enlisted men. If we consider that, in contrast to replacements from Germany, new units had not been properly selected and suffered heavily from acclimatization (sickness levels reached their peak in September–October 1942, with an average of 20 per cent of men falling ill), one can imagine how heavy the burden on the 'old' Afrikakorps units must have been.

At this stage the overall quality of the replacements had also become an issue. In the period between 21 May and 20 September 1942 the 21. Panzer-Division reported an overall loss of 5,695 men compared with a total intake of 2,612 replacements (207 officers and 2,405 other ranks). Even though by 21 September the division had a nominal strength of 8,218, its actual combat strength was only 6,748. Even worse, half of the replacements were unsatisfactorily trained soldiers and the other half were sick or wounded soldiers, veterans of the Eastern Front who had volunteered for service in North Africa and who were sent there after recovering. Apparently, selection did not work in their case, and acclimatization in the desert during summer took a very heavy toll with up to 30–40 per cent of the replacements getting sick and being hospitalized. Problems were also experienced in the overall quality of both NCOs and combat troops. Amongst the former there were many who had been serving so far in replacement and administrative units at home and thus lacked both front-line experience and training with modern weapons. For the latter, most men proved simply unsuitable for front-line duties and consequently there were shortages in tank commanders, group and platoon leaders, riflemen, gunners and radio communication specialists. The only available solution was to fill these gaps (in at least half of cases) with men who had both front-line and desert combat experience, while every third driver was a soldier lacking the required licence. An overall picture of the situation is best given by Rommel's own words:

> Of the German elements of the Panzer Army, 17,000 men had been in action in Africa ever since the beginning of the campaign, and all of them had suffered more or less severely from the effects of the climate… The German divisions (now numbering four) were short of a further 17,000 men, caused by death, sickness, wounds and, above all, the very low unit strength with which they had started. Hence, our problems were also very serious in the field of personnel.

If we compare the Afrikakorps' total strength in August 1942 with the above figures, less than 30 per cent (and this figure is likely to have dropped further, since others would have been sent back to Germany before the Alamein

A group of Afrikakorps *Schützen* (or *Panzergrenadiere*, as mechanized infantry were renamed in July 1942) having a moment of rest under the shade of a truck after a victorious clash with British forces (note the Valentine tank in the background). This is a heavy machine-gun team made up of veterans, judging by the sun-bleached uniforms. It is not clear what armband the soldier in the background is wearing. (US National Archives)

A mixed German and Italian police patrol in the rear. The Afrikakorps Feldgendarmerie (military police) are wearing, other than the peculiar gorget and 'Feldgendarmerie' cuff title, Dutch-made pith helmets. The Italians are from the Polizia dell'Africa Italiana (PAI), the Italian African police. (Piero Crociani archive)

battle in October) of the Afrikakorps soldiers were old-timer '*Afrikaner*', or long-serving veterans of the desert war. Quite clearly, in the summer of 1942 the Afrikakorps was no longer quite as it had been in the previous spring or in 1941, and the inevitable consequences are easy to imagine. The situation did not improve at all in the months to follow, and it actually got worse after the defeat at El Alamein in October–November 1942. In the period between 21 September and 31 December 1942 the 21. Panzer–Division reported a total loss of approximately 4,000 men (including more than 2,200 sick) while, in comparison, a total of 988 replacements were received during the same period. On 15 December 1942 the division had a combat strength of less than 1,600. Divisions would be brought up to strength again after the final retreat to the Mareth Line, but by then what was left was a shadow of the early Afrikakorps.

TRAINING

In early 1941 both the 5. leichte and the 15. Panzer-Divisionen possessed a good level of training. This was thanks to the intensive training undertaken by Panzer units since the summer of 1940, which took place alongside a major reorganization process, and which took advantage of experience gained during the campaign against France in May–June 1940. The large number of battle-experienced personnel available also guaranteed a high level of training, regardless of how many young, inexperienced recruits the units had. This does not mean, however, that their training was entirely suitable or adequate for North Africa. The January 1941 training programme for the 15. Panzer-Division did include several relevant subjects such as developing fire plans for the attack,

Personal hygiene was important in the desert. Here an Afrikakorps soldier checks his hair outside a tent quarter. Note that his shorts are longer than the German-issue ones and are apparently either captured from the British or Italian issue. (HITM)

achieving and exploiting an armoured breakthrough, cooperation in the field between armour and artillery, field reconnaissance, long-range and land-to-air communications and redeployment at night. On the other hand, all this was intended for fighting in Europe and particular emphasis was placed on fighting in urban and in wooded areas, both of which were extremely scarce in the Western Desert. The only kind of training given to soldiers before leaving for North Africa was a series of lectures given by travellers and specialists in desert hygiene, which resulted only in creating confusion amongst Afrikakorps soldiers who arrived in Libya with completely misguided ideas about the actual effects the environmental conditions would have on them – especially heat, insects and hygiene. Only instructions concerning hygiene would prove to be correct and therefore useful.

Orientation was soon discovered to be the real problem; in Europe soldiers were used to relying on reference points and maps, and they soon discovered that there were none of the former in the Western Desert. The consequences of this were soon apparent when a large convoy of supply trucks sent to reach the units advancing toward Tobruk in April 1941 became lost (trucks were still found wandering in the desert after a week) and, in the months to follow, with the 5. leichte and the 15. Panzer divisions bumping into one another during a night march. As Hauptmann Daumillier emphasized in a report of October 1941, one of the greatest problems troops had to face in the desert was orientation; as he put it, it was practically impossible to keep a route using only a compass, the tachometer and the map. What actually saved many of the Afrikakorps soldiers during the first advance into Cyrenaica in April 1941 was the fact that, once they realized they were lost, they could always turn northwards and march until they reached the Via Balbia, the only paved road stretching all along the coast.

A large Afrikakorps depot, with a Horch staff car at the centre. Bringing supplies from Tripoli harbour to the front in Cyrenaica was a time- and fuel-consuming task; in most cases they had to be transported by lorries following the Via Balbia. (Carlo Pecchi collection)

Practical training in the field for soldiers of a communication unit. The training officer, sheltered under the tent, is lecturing on the use of radios to soldiers seated under the sun. This kind of training became more and more frequent in early 1942, when Afrikakorps units underwent extensive retraining for desert operations. (HITM)

Experience was gained during the 1941 campaign in North Africa, but apparently there still were no opportunities to retrain Afrikakorps units during that year, and this experience was instead put to use to train replacements back in Germany. A training manual for units destined for the desert existed from June 1940, but on 8 June 1941 the German Army's chief of staff requested new directives for the training of replacements for the Afrikakorps. Given the harsh conditions of fighting in desert areas, and since experience had shown how units tended to split into small groups during fighting, changes were introduced to training. These included a strengthening of both the physical and mental condition of the soldiers destined to join the Afrikakorps, and also a specific training programme aimed at avoiding the concentration of both men and vehicles. The smaller, ideal *Kampfgruppe* (battle group) was to be composed of one or two machine-gun groups and an anti-tank group armed with either anti-tank guns or rifles. Large allowances of hand grenades, mines, etc., were required, and soldiers had to learn to react quickly to enemy attacks, to scan the battlefield and report promptly to their superiors, and to be able to launch impromptu shock attacks. Training directives were issued shortly thereafter in mid-July 1941, which included a mixture of healthcare precautions for the desert and a variety of directives. These ranged from formal training for recruits (which was to include as many bivouacs in the open as possible) to combat training, which aimed at enhancing performance when fighting in small groups and making sure that extreme care was taken in the maintenance of weapons, ammunition and equipment.

As early as 1 May 1941 the Afrikakorps had ordered the creation of a *Feldersatz Bataillon* ('field replacement battalion'), which was aimed at gathering together the replacements coming from Germany and giving them specific further training, as well as getting them acquainted with both the environment and the new units they would be assigned to. Working for both divisions, it was made up of three companies, only one of which was for the replacements of 5. leichte-Division. Actual training of replacements in Germany during 1941 seems to have been adequate, but again lacking the required emphasis on living and fighting in the desert. Otto Henning, a volunteer with Aufklärungs-Abteilung 3, joined his training unit on 15 August 1941 and immediately began his basic training. This included ground exercises, weapons and fire exercises, theoretical lessons and training with armoured cars. Eventually he undertook specific training with AFVs (armoured fighting vehicles), which required each crew member to be able to fulfil every duty aboard, and on 1 March 1942 he reached North Africa. No mention is made in his memoirs of any specific training for the desert, and his company was immediately sent to join its parent unit without any kind of acclimatization or further training.

As a matter of fact it was only in early 1942 that a widespread training programme was started amongst Afrikakorps units. An initial order on the matter was issued on 15 February 1942 by the headquarters of Panzerarmee Afrika and included such topics as disciplinary procedures (soldiers always had to salute), officers' care for their soldiers, training with heavy weapons, training of infantry units in defensive positions, training of reconnaissance units (now required to work alongside anti-tank guns) to improve their initiative, training for anti-tank gunners to improve their skills and capabilities, training for field artillery in mobility and observation, training of anti-aircraft

An anti-aircraft MG 34 mounted on the back of an Opel Blitz medium lorry, with a large ammunition feeding and cartridge-case recovery drum at the bottom. The 20mm anti-aircraft gun, also motorized on its half-tracked mount, was a much more effective gun. (US National Archives)

guns to fight every kind of ground target (not only tanks) and, for all units, specific training in night marches and in the care and maintenance of weapons and equipment. On 20 February Afrikakorps headquarters issued its own orders for a comprehensive training programme, applying to all units and to every single soldier regardless of his rank. A particular emphasis was placed on two specific matters: command and leadership for the officers, and the new 'more weapons, less men' organization, which required a more comprehensive training aimed at enabling every soldier to cover every kind of duty. In particular, infantry soldiers were required not only to be able to operate every kind of infantry weapon, but also to be able to serve as gun crews if needed. Training courses for the officers included theoretical exercises and lectures, which included a series of 'war games' to improve familiarity with both terrain and procedures, and a series of regular lessons to be held with the troops, with the aim of keeping them constantly informed and therefore keeping their spirits high. Orientation in the field, in particular the capability to recognize targets quickly (even when moving) and to move toward them was another important issue, which also required an improvement in navigation skills and the use of the compass. Officers and drivers were taught not to undertake any easy detour, and also always to prepare and check their equipment, the compass above all. The right course was to be continuously checked using both the compass and the tachometer, being always ready to get back to a known position as soon as one realized one had become lost (otherwise, one was to drive toward the position of friendly units using the compass). Unless required by tactical needs, there was to be no movement at night or in a sandstorm, though this rule was amended to enable the Afrikakorps to perform its flanking movement around the Gazala Line during the night.

Orders concerning training issued for individual units added further details. An order given by the headquarters of the 21. Panzer-Division dated 20 February 1942 stressed the need for the Panzer regiment to improve

A portable wireless transmitter/receiver position in the desert, made up of two packs (one consisting of the wireless set, the other of the battery and accessories case). These were available in two different basic versions: one with a range of 4–15km, and another more powerful one with a range of 10–25km. (HITM)

combined-arms warfare and cooperation with other units, which included fire and movement procedures that required tank commanders to observe the result of their fire and order appropriate changes with the aim of achieving actual hits, rather than merely attempting general fire in order to sap the morale of enemy units. Infantry – now undergoing a complete reorganization with infantry companies including anti-tank guns – were trained to serve as a security force for the division, creating strongholds capable of withstanding enemy counter-attacks when needed. An order from the headquarters of the 15. Panzer-Division dated 23 April 1942 greatly emphasized the need for flexibility in order to face the constantly changing situation on the battlefield; units had to be ready to attack either with their vehicles or on foot, with or without tank support. The Panzer regiment, in particular, was to be trained to move and attack in close order, with the aim of delivering and exploiting the decisive blow against the enemy forces. Every single company was to report about progress made, which would be checked. Regarding night marches, specific training was required with the leading units trained in spotting tracks and keeping the correct course, which was to be marked using burning captured oil canisters. The follow-up units were trained in following them while being also able to recognize their actual position. Subordination of astronomical measurement units to the divisions, which were also required to train selected navigation officers, greatly helped in this particular task.

Truck-borne personnel during a lull in the desert fighting. Note the different shades of colour of the *Einheitsfeldmütze*, ranging from brand new to sun-bleached. Generally speaking this would indicate the difference between veterans and green replacements. (HITM)

Only after September 1942, with the lull on the Alamein front, were new orders concerning training issued. This was a consequence of the large intake of new replacements, who were partly untrained or undertrained, and also as a consequence of the new tasks the divisions had to face, which were now aimed mainly at manning and defending a line against the enemy offensive. This again required a widespread training programme at every level. For example, the 21. Panzer-Division had to train not only single men, with an emphasis on the training of NCOs and officer candidates, but also individual units ranging from platoon to company and battalion level. Although the basic tactical principles ruling training remained unvaried, some changes are noteworthy; tank crews were now required to execute in battle the movements they had practised during drills with absolute and unconditional discipline, which meant a severe curtailment of that flexibility that had made possible many of the Afrikakorps' victories. The consequences of poorer training and overall quality of troops, and also of the different demands of the battlefield, are made clear by the new training instructions for the reconnaissance units; while in the past they were trained to exploit situations using their own strength, now the emphasis was placed on the motto 'see much, don't be seen'. The fact that new drivers now completely skipped theoretical schooling is just another indicator of how much the situation had changed when compared with the earlier Afrikakorps.

APPEARANCE AND EQUIPMENT

By 1940 the German Army, later followed by other branches, had developed a desert uniform and desert equipment for its troops. It was designed at the Tropical Institute of Hamburg, and eventually saw widespread use even outside North Africa, the area where it was first intended for use. This explains how it was possible to quickly dress and equip Afrikakorps units in early 1941, even though the first units of 5. leichte-Division set out for North Africa still dressed in their European *Feldgrau* uniform, which they exchanged with their desert one only once en route to Tripoli (apparently the Italians were concerned about having these men going around in their shorts). In a way, the German desert uniform was quite innovative and introduced certain unique

 AFRIKAKORPS INFANTRYMAN, 'WINTER BATTLE', 1941

This *Obergefreiter* (senior corporal) is from a motorized infantry unit during the *Crusader* battle, and is a veteran of North Africa. His helmet, where the sand goggles are worn, is painted in a sandy colour, and he wears a very useful scarf at his neck . He wears the standard desert uniform worn by Afrikakorps soldiers, though the sun has bleached its original greenish colour. Rank, collar and eagle insignia for the desert uniform are shown (**1**). He wears the standard infantryman's webbing with the desert belt and suspenders, and his equipment includes the cartridge pouches for his Karabiner 98K rifle as well as spade and bayonet with leather webbing; stick hand grenades are tucked into his belt. Viewed from the rear (**2**), the equipment is reduced to a minimum and includes the spade with the bayonet attached (with canvas webbing), the bread bag, two canteens and the gas-mask canister. The model 24 *Stielhandgranate* (**3**) is shown here with the explosive head and the security cap removed, revealing both the detonator and the porcelain ball used to ignite it. The writing on the detached head is an abbreviation of '*Nebel Handgranate*' (smoke grenade). This, along with the white line running around the head, distinguishes it from an explosive grenade. The soldier's canteen, carrying his daily water ration, is shown here with the cup removed and put over a camp stove, with its fuel and matches shown in detail, ready to make some coffee or tea (**4**).

1

2

3

4

peculiarities in German Army field dress. Its elements included the pith helmet (*Tropenhelm*) made of compressed cork (Dutch ones were also issued), the olive cotton cloth field cap (*Feldmütze*) and the olive canvas material peaked field cap (*Einheitsfeldmütze*). The European steel helmet was retained, eventually being camouflaged in a sandy colour.

The uniform, also made of olive lightweight cotton material, consisted of a jacket or blouse (*Feldbluse*) that was open at the collar and cut in the same style as the European *Feldgrau* jacket, and of three different kinds of trousers all with a built-in cloth belt: long trousers (*lange Hosen*), desert breeches (*Stiefelhosen*, not intended for mounted personnel, and worn with high boots) and shorts (*kurze Hosen*) cut high at the thighs. There was only one version of the desert shirt, in lightweight olive cotton, with four buttons (it could be worn with a necktie), long sleeves, two breast pockets and loops for shoulder straps. A double-breasted greatcoat, made of dark brown woollen cloth and cut in the same style as the *Feldgrau* one, was issued for warmth on the cold desert nights. The only variation was the desert version of the motorcyclists' coat, intended to protect men from rain, made of heavy olive cotton twill material. Leather greatcoats, used only by generals and high-ranking officers, also saw use. Footwear included desert high boots with leather soles and toecaps and knee-high olive green laced canvas, and the short ankle boots (*Schnürschuhe*, or laced shoes), made of the same stuff and cut in the same design. Afrikakorps soldiers would often modify the former into the latter by cutting off the knee-high canvas.

Every soldier bound for North Africa was issued a desert uniform kit that included (amongst other things) one pith helmet, one *Feldmütze* and one *Einheitsfeldmütze*, two uniform jackets, one long and one short pair of

Soldiers from Aufklärungs-Abteilung 33 posing for a photograph. The unit is denoted by the insignia worn on the European *Einheitsfeldmütze* by the officer on the right. The Knight's Cross wearer at centre is possibly Oberst Erwin Menny, who was temporary commander of the division in December 1941. (HITM)

trousers, one greatcoat, three shirts, three vests, one long and three short pairs of underpants, four pairs of socks, two sets of pyjamas and three blankets. Officers were permitted to obtain a single tailor-made desert uniform including a *Feldmütze*, a jacket, breeches, long trousers and a greatcoat (this uniform was paid for by the army and retained by the wearer). Equipment consisted of a mixture of desert items, which were of the same style as the European ones, and those already in use with the European *Feldgrau* uniform. The desert belt gives a practical example of the changes introduced to the normal equipment; the use of leather, unsuitable in arid climates, was avoided and it was replaced by canvas and webbing of a brown olive, reed green, sand, tan or light brown colour; metal components were also painted in olive. Thus the desert belt was made of webbed fabric about 4.5cm wide, with the normal buckle already in use with the *Feldgrau* uniform attached. A belt with a round buckle was also issued, for use by officers, who often would rather use the simple frame 'two-hook' brown leather belt of the *Feldgrau* uniform.

The basic equipment infantry soldiers carried included support suspenders (or 'Y' straps), also made of canvas or webbing, to which the desert version of the harness (or assault pack) could be attached. Riflemen had brown leather ammunition pouches for the Karabiner 98k, while for the MP 38/40 machine pistol a desert version of the three-magazine pouch was issued. Bayonet web frogs were also made either of leather or olive-coloured webbing, with all frogs in the desert having a securing strap. Desert versions of the bread bag, the rucksack and the hand-grenade bag were also made, whilst only details (like the use of canvas and webbing or of olive-coloured fabrics) were changed for the entrenching tool, the canteen and the cup. No changes, other than the addition of sand-coloured paint, were made to the mess kit and the gas-mask canister. The camouflaged tent quarter (*Zeltbahn*) used in Europe saw also widespread use in North Africa.

Some personal items specifically made for use in desert areas became quite common amongst Afrikakorps soldiers. These included scarves used to protect oneself from sand, olive-coloured sweaters (though the European grey ones were also used), gloves and a wide variety of sun and dust goggles, which were very popular. It is worth noting that the use of canvas and webbing does not necessarily denote items produced specifically for use in the desert, since these also saw much use later in the war. Indeed, the hasty redeployment of units to North Africa during the summer of 1942, and later in Tunisia, saw widespread use of the European *Feldgrau* uniform items.

One of the most interesting matters relating to the German desert uniforms is the lack of any difference between ranks; the basic uniform was intended for use by officers, NCOs and enlisted men without distinction. Even insignia did not change; the standard-issue uniform included a breast eagle and lapel badges (*Litzen*) in a mouse grey or bluish-grey thread on an olive, khaki or tan backing, which were common to all ranks. Desert versions of the shoulder straps were made for enlisted men and NCOs, the latter retaining their characteristic braid (made of light-brown cotton) around the collar. The shoulder straps, made from the same material as the jacket, could also be worn on the first version of the desert shirt. However, officers did retain some distinction by commonly using the same insignias worn on the *Feldgrau* European uniform. Shoulder straps, the only item intended for use on desert uniforms, were basically the same but made of a silver-coloured soutache braid. These were plain (for junior officers), interwoven (for senior officers) or gold- and silver-coloured for generals. These could be worn on

A group of Afrikakorps soldiers resting in Libya, early 1941. Their general appearance and the use of the pith helmet suggest the early date. It is worth noting the arrangement of the weapons and the Red Cross armband worn by the first soldier on the left. (HITM)

either the jacket or the shirt, and they had a coloured backing denoting the wearer's branch of service (they were also worn on NCOs' and enlisted men's shoulder straps as piping). Not intended for wear with the colonial uniform were both the breast eagle and the lapel badges, which were made of silver-coloured metallic threads sewn onto a dark blue-green backing, which was thicker than that normally used for desert uniforms. Within the lapel badges were stripes with the colour of the service branch to which the soldier belonged. These were worn on the desert uniform in the same positions as the original badges, with the eagle's swastika often overlapping the top flap of the pocket.

A peculiar insignia of the Afrikakorps were the 'Afrikakorps' and 'Afrika' cuff titles. The former was introduced on 18 July 1941 and could be worn by all personnel on the right forearm of their jacket and greatcoat; it was

awarded after two months' service in North Africa or a shorter period for those who were wounded. This was a unique case in the German Army of a unit cuff title being shared by all the members of a corps and Panzer army; generally these were reserved for smaller units. It was only later in the war that the 'Grossdeutschland' cuff title would share the same role, and only following the reorganization of the unit as a corps. The 'Afrika' cuff title was introduced on 15 January 1943 in order to replace the 'Afrikakorps' one, and it was no longer intended to mark the distinction of belonging to a unit but rather more as a campaign decoration. It was awarded to those who had served for six months in North Africa, or a shorter period for those who were wounded or had fallen sick.

Only minor variations were introduced to the desert uniforms of the Afrikakorps from the German Army staff and the manufacturers. After 1942 a new jacket was introduced without a pleated breast and side pockets (flaps retained their shape), while the new shirt no longer had loops for the shoulder straps. Also, both the *Feldmütze* and the *Einheitsfeldmütze* lost the inverted 'V' soutache or branch of service colour worn above the national cockade, while retaining the silver lining for officers. The normal practice saw a more relaxed attitude toward uniforms and dressing than might have been envisaged; the use of Italian (particularly the much sought-after 'sahariana' jacket) and of British pieces of uniform became quite common, in the latter case especially after the capture of large stocks at Tobruk in June 1942 (British shorts were longer and more comfortable than the German ones). All through the campaign in North Africa there was a certain slackening in the dress attitude of Afrikakorps soldiers, which brought some rebukes from the corps and Rommel's own

Improvisation, in this case using captured equipment pressed into Afrikakorps service, was one of the main distinguishing features of the German forces in the desert. A British Bren-Gun Carrier has been upgraded by mounting a Hotchkiss 25mm SA 34 anti-tank gun, a weapon that was quite useless against modern armour. (HITM)

command. Soon certain items like the pith helmet were discarded by front-line troops, though it was still used to some extent by those serving in rear areas and by vehicle crews.

Checking supplies and storage in the desert. Especially in the summer of 1942, after the seizure of Tobruk, the Afrikakorps relied to a large extent on captured British supplies, clothing and equipment. Note how these soldiers wear longer shorts than the Afrikakorps standard-issue ones, indicating that they were probably captured. (HITM)

The German desert uniform, developed on the basis of the knowledge and experiences gained in the German colonies in eastern Africa before and during World War I, soon revealed some inadequacies. Hauptmann Daumillier's report of 31 October 1941 stressed the fact that both the trousers and the desert breeches were inadequate because of their shape, and that it was thanks only to soldiers' ingenuity that a suitable solution was found, as they had adapted their trousers to be worn over the laced shoes and tightened at the hem. Even the jacket was deficient, being too tight, uncomfortable to wear and therefore very unpopular, while the material used for uniforms and caps bleached very fast and eventually became quite visible on the ground (the same effect was observed with new uniforms, though in this case because their colour was too dark). The extent to which the Germans were unprepared for the desert is also demonstrated by a lack of mosquito nets. The situation worsened with time and experience; uniforms washed in sea water shrank, not to mention the fact that the fabric they were made of (which was overly heavy) offered little if any protection against the rocky terrain or the sand. It was also inadequate against the cold nights and hot days. In 1942 the desert breeches were no longer in use, while those who could happily exchanged their German shorts (which were too short and worn only during periods of rest or in the rear areas) with British ones. Even the popular and appreciated *Einheitsfeldmütze* had its shortcomings and some alterations were required, namely a leather perspiration band. The greatcoat proved useful against the cold at night, but it was too short and hampered movement. Only the laced

A staff unit prepares to move to another position. Interestingly, the odd mixture of uniforms denotes how individuals responded to the climate; the one seated in the back of the car to the right wears an overcoat, others wear their jacket and two more are either in shirtsleeve order or in shorts only. The man walking to the left of the image has an Italian 'sahariana' jacket. (HITM)

shoes turned out to be a good and suitable solution (several variants were produced up to 1942), and unsurprisingly soldiers would cut off the top portion of the high boots, turning them into laced shoes.

In contrast to uniform, equipment (particularly for infantrymen) proved adequate and suitable. The reason for this was that, because it was modelled on that in use with the European *Feldgrau* uniform, men were already accustomed to it, and the use of canvas or webbing proved to be a good choice (it was also adopted later in the war). There were only a few remarks of criticism, which were about the Bakelite components of certain items, such as the canteen's cup, which were too fragile. It is interesting to note that both the Luftwaffe and the SS would develop desert uniforms, or parts of uniform, for their own men, which proved better both in their cut (the SS one was made like the Italian 'sahariana') and in the fabric used, though it must be added that their actual use was quite limited in comparison with the Afrikakorps uniform.

 MAJOR, STAFF HEADQUARTERS, 1942

This *Major* shows the typical arrangement of the desert uniform for officers of the Afrikakorps. Although there were no differences between the uniforms and insignia of officers, NCOs and enlisted men (generals would mostly wear tailor-made uniforms), Afrikakorps officers found a way to distinguish themselves by using the insignia from the *Feldgrau* European uniform. This officer wears an officers' *Einheitsfeldmütze* still with the inverted 'V' soutache, in this case white, denoting infantry. He also wears the Knight's Cross at the neck of his shirt, with the 1941-model jacket with European insignia, the 'Afrikakorps' cuff title on the right arm and, on his chest, several decorations including the Iron Cross first class, a wound badge and the infantry assault badge (*Infanterie Sturmabzeichen*) on the left pocket. He wears the simple European 'two-hook' leather belt. His shorts, longer than the German desert ones, are captured from either Italian or British stocks. Details show the European-style eagle, lapel and shoulder badges and insignia (**1**), the wound badge (**2**), the Iron Cross second class with its ribbon (**3**), the infantry assault badge (**4**), the new 1942-model *Einheitsfeldmütze* for other ranks, which lacked the soutache (**5**), an officer's compass (a very important item in the desert) (**6**), a standard pair of field binoculars (**7**) and a 'Daimon' electric torch (**8**), which could be tucked into a pocket, with its three colour filters.

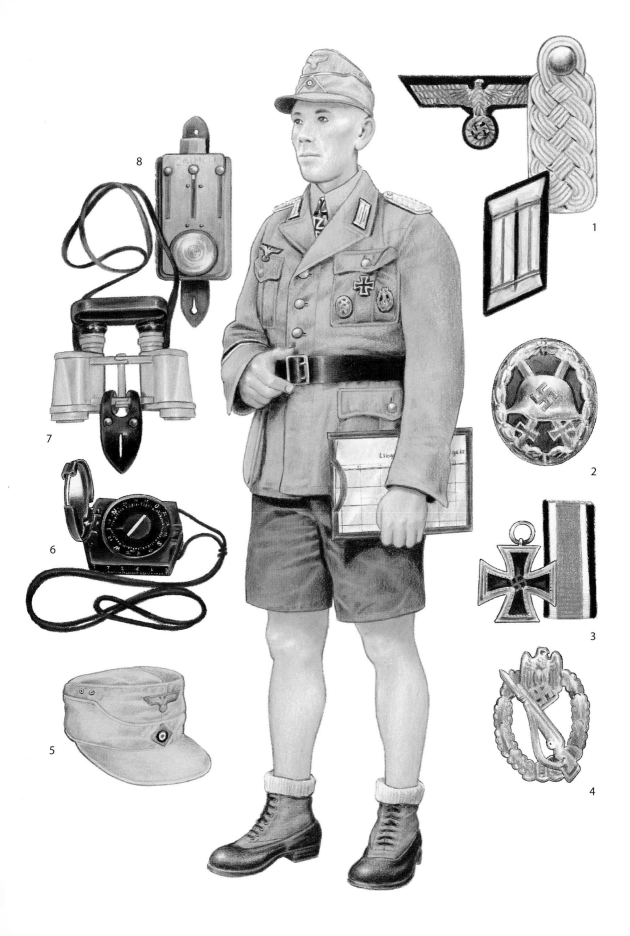

LIFE ON CAMPAIGN

Terrain and climate were crucial factors in the life of Afrikakorps soldiers, as they were for all forces fighting in North Africa. Until the summer of 1942, when the war moved into Egypt, the arena of fighting was the Libyan region of Cyrenaica, or more specifically eastern Cyrenaica and the Egyptian border. Fighting took place in western Cyrenaica only for brief periods, dominated in its northern part by the massif of the 'green mountains'. Between April and November 1941 and May and June 1942 the fighting was concentrated in the area between Gazala in the west and Sollum and Halfaya Pass to the east. The striking difference between western and eastern Cyrenaica is easy to understand if we look at a simple piece of data: in Benghazi to the west there was up to 270mm of rain in a year, but only 160mm farther east in Tobruk. The latter, being a major harbour, dominated eastern Cyrenaica in terms of strategic importance. Impassable cliffs running along the coast restricted movement, and in turn made positions such as Halfaya Pass strategically important. On the other hand, even if large units hardly ever ventured more than 100km away from the coastline, the open desert terrain lacked any other significant obstacles such as rivers or cities and it proved to be highly suitable for armoured and mechanized warfare. One major hindrance, however, was the lack of roads; apart from the paved Via Balbia running along the coast, the whole area contained only tracks running across the desert at best, which heavy vehicles could only sometimes make use of. Orientation was a major hurdle, since crossing the desert could cause one to lose one's sense of direction, and even tracks could easily lead to a different place than supposed. The situation was worse in Egypt, which contained a desert more arid than that of Cyrenaica and which was dominated only by the Qattara Depression to the south.

The aspect of desert life that most affected the men of the Afrikakorps was undoubtedly the harsh climate; with temperatures sometimes rising up to 75°C (the average stood at about 50°C) much difficulty was encountered when forces clashed during the summer months. In years past, during periods of colonial warfare, fighting was restricted to the cooler winter season. Physical fitness was a basic prerequisite for service in the region, and men aged under 35 were best suited for service. Even so, the intense heat would often have a paralysing effect on the unaccustomed soldier, further aggravating any disease caused by poor diet and hygiene. During rest and lull periods, to avoid the heat of the noon hours, three hours of rest without any physical activity were allowed. It was at this time of the day that cold rations were served, while hot rations were served during the cold nights (when temperatures fell below 0°C). The extremes of temperature soldiers encountered within a single 24-hour period were aggravating. Hans von Luck, serving in 1942 with a motorized infantry battalion of the 21. Panzer-Division, recalled how they used to wear the greatcoat (necessary during the night) and thick scarves until well into the morning. Slowly, the heat would make its way through them, and at that point they had to be taken off. Gradually, during the day, the heat would become more and more unbearable until the midday pause. The popular image of soldiers frying bacon and eggs on the heated armoured plating of a Panzer, as shown by propaganda newsreels, seems to have been subject to quite a debate. Luck wrote that it did really happen, and that he did it himself; others revealed that it was some kind of a trick for propaganda purposes, with the armour plating having been heated using an oxy-hydrogen flame. The truth can probably be discerned from a simple remark from the history of Panzer-Regiment 5: watching the newsreel, its veterans could only think how hard it had been to get hold of a few eggs, not to mention bacon.

Sand and the ever-present dust added further strain on men and equipment; even without the terrible sandstorms, wind and even gentle breezes would throw up into the air extremely fine sand, against which soldiers could not possibly fully protect themselves. Sandstorms, raised by the *ghibli*, the desert wind, were amongst the most annoying and dangerous problems; when the *ghibli* blew from the south it could raise the temperature up to 50°C or more, and it could blow all day long and change its direction very suddenly. Worst of all, it could raise sandstorms up to 2–3m in height, against which the only available protection (goggles, scarves, etc.) was quite useless.

As well as heavily affecting weapons, vehicles and equipment, the desert climate could often have a severely detrimental effect on morale and psychological well-being. Climate had a variable impact upon the various troops of the Afrikakorps; it was one thing to serve in rear areas, especially at headquarters, but for front-line troops the situation was much worse, especially for tank crews who suffered heavily from the heat. From the point of view of the Afrikakorps soldiers, many of whom had been attracted by the idea of the climate while at home, the desert offered only sandstorms, swarms of flies and a disconsolate monotony. The popular and idyllic images of palms, oases, Arabs and colonial towns with their white houses were a common sight only to troops serving in rear areas. For most of the Afrikakorps soldiers it was only the desert, day after day, with all its inconveniences and discomforts.

Soldiers resting under the shade of a Hanomag SdKfz 11 tractor, used to tow light artillery and anti-tank guns. For the men of the Afrikakorps there was hardly any protection against the relentless African sun other than the shade provided by vehicles or tarpaulins, like the one wrapped around the cabin of this vehicle. (Carlo Pecchi collection)

Food was another sore point; on paper this was to be supplied by the Italians, who proved eventually unable to supply any foodstuff with a high nutritional value such as ham, eggs, butter and evaporated milk. Large quantities of food had to be supplied directly from Germany, and even then there was not much thought given to this otherwise sensitive matter. Nobody seemed to care about the fact that some foodstuffs just happen to be less wholesome in arid climates than they are in Europe, or that others, like potatoes, could be canned, as was customary in the British Army. Ease of transportation was, on the other hand, much more important; thus the soldiers of the Afrikakorps got in 1941 large amounts of pulses, canned meat and sausages, while only once a week did they receive rice, semolina, barley,

This is what a march in the North African desert looked like from the ground: a vast, empty horizon with virtually no reference points, where at best only the dust clouds raised by other vehicles could be seen. Orientation on the ground was therefore essential. (HITM)

A field kitchen mounted on a truck, which gave it a certain degree of mobility. Given the very mobile kind of warfare fought in the Western Desert, supplies were not always able to keep up with combat units. As a consequence, many combat units experienced problems with food supplies and had to resort to eating combat rations. (Carlo Pecchi collection)

porridge oats and other farinaceous food. Until August 1941 there was no butter at all, and later on it would have been available only occasionally, along with other fresh items like fish, vegetables (only dried ones were available), fruit and potatoes. Eventually, some items had to be entirely replaced; in place of butter soldiers got pilchards' oil that, while a delicacy in Europe, was nauseating when served in temperatures of about 50°C. Canned meat was also supplied in large quantities by the Italians and eaten cold. Cans bore the letters 'AM' for Amministrazione Militare (military administration), and were soon given the name 'Alter Mann' (old man) or 'Asinus Mussolini' (Mussolini's Ass). They were made of fat, cartilage and sinews. Tuna, cheese, liver sausage and pork were also part of the very monotonous diet of the

Purchasing eggs and other foodstuffs from the locals. In general the relationship between Afrikakorps soldiers and the Arabs was good, with the latter providing items otherwise hard to obtain, though mostly at very high prices. (HITM)

Afrikakorps soldiers, along with the Italian canned meat. Attempts to make the food more palatable failed owing to the inadequacy of available freezing facilities. Bread was another problem since until summer 1941 there was only a single bakery company in North Africa, which was unable to supply all the German troops. Moreover, German bakeries, designed to use wood as fuel (which was quite scarce in the area), had to be modified to use coal, which turned into another supply requirement. Long-life bread had to be supplied directly from Germany for several months, though by spring 1942 bakery companies were able to work at full capacity in spite of the constant lack of water. The situation was such that in November 1942 bread rations were curtailed from 375g of fresh bread a day to 250g a day, and this of the long-life variety.

The lack of variety in diet was a problem, since the diet of Afrikakorps soldiers hardly altered day after day, week after week and month after month.

A field kitchen in the desert, ready to prepare the daily meal for soldiers of an Afrikakorps unit. These kitchens were designed to burn wood, and had to be converted for the use of coal. (HITM)

Indeed, a change would occur only when stocks of British food were captured, which were much-welcome booty. Strange as it may sound today, Italian food was seldom welcome, especially when German soldiers ate it in the Italian messes; these were strictly divided by rank, with officers receiving macaroni with tomato sauce, olive oil and meat; NCOs receiving macaroni with tomato and olive oil; and enlisted men receiving only macaroni with tomato. Trade with the local Arabs could provide only a few additional eggs or a melon, and at very high prices. Vitamins could be gained only by eating lemons and drinking lemonade, and these were at least supplied in large quantities, while it was only seldom that marmalades or jams (mainly supplied by the Italians) were available, if at all. In addition, the actual quantity of food available was at times inadequate, and there were times (such as the period between June and August 1941 or July and August 1942) when inadequate supplies,

 AFRIKAKORPS SOLDIERS DURING A REST PERIOD, TRIPOLITANIA 1941

Afrikakorps soldiers did not serve only at the front; there were several rear-area units and headquarters spread across both Tripolitania and Cyrenaica, and occasionally soldiers were granted temporary leave to places such as Tripoli and Benghazi. In such cases soldiers were required to wear the full formal desert uniform of the Afrikakorps, which in some cases would need to be supplied to them again. This group of soldiers shows a mixture of green replacements just arrived in Libya being led by an Afrikakorps veteran, an *Unteroffizier* (corporal) who is wearing the *Einheitsfeldmütze* along with the 'Afrikakorps' cuff title (awarded after two months' service in North Africa), along with the ribbon of the Iron Cross second class. Following his example, the *Gefreiter* is also wearing the *Einheitsfeldmütze*. The Feldgendarmerie, or military police, were active in North Africa; detachments were assigned to divisions and others served in the rear areas, their purpose being to control the German soldiers, at times along with the Italian police who had limited powers when dealing with members of the Afrikakorps. The uniform of the Feldgendarmerie in North Africa did not differ from the basic Afrikakorps one, apart from the use of the 'Feldgendarmerie' cuff title on the left arm and the wearing of the gorget. Occasionally European shoulder straps and lapel badges sporting the characteristic orange arm-of-service colour would be used as well.

widespread theft and the difficulties supply convoys faced in reaching front-line units resulted in hunger amongst the troops.

The terrain and climate, with the intense heat and the sand, together with inadequate uniforms and nutrition all contributed to the spread of disease and sickness amongst Afrikakorps soldiers. Even if this was not a real problem during the early months, after the summer and autumn of 1941 the ever-increasing cases of sickness would reveal the full extent of the issue. In the autumn of 1941 a thorough analysis of the cases of sickness was carried out, concluding that diet was to a greater or lesser extent responsible for it. Legumes and pork (in particular bacon, lard and sausages) affected the already exhausted intestines of the soldiers, who were in large part suffering from dysentery and jaundice. After a few weeks of service in North Africa, soldiers were generally found to have suffered from a loss of about ten per cent of their weight. Diet was not the only source of disease however. The wearing of woollen belly bands (waist bands intended to protect the belly), necessary to withstand the harsh extremes of climate during night and day, was not compulsory until later during the campaign, a fact that also contributed to the spread of intestinal diseases. Insects, in particular the plague of flies and mosquitoes, also played their part; other than spreading epidemics, the constant presence of these swarms became a heavy burden for soldiers who had to fight against them constantly, particularly while eating. They were not easily dealt with, as they stuck to every part of the body, including the mouth, nose and eyes. A dentist's surgery in Derna eventually found a solution to the problem by obtaining a chameleon to keep the flies away.

Staff officers in shirtsleeve order in discussion, taking shelter behind a stone wall. They are all wearing the first type of Afrikakorps shirt with attachments for the shoulder straps (with European ones attached) and the first version of the *Einheitsfeldmütze*, still bearing the inverted 'V' above the national cockade. (HITM)

One measure that had to be undertaken to prevent the spreading of infections transmitted by flies was the use of boxed latrines, with a rudimentary anti-insect wick, though hardly any kind of prevention was possible at all for front-line troops, especially during combat. Another problem was the lack of medical units and facilities in the early stages of the campaign. As much as 70 per cent of the medical equipment for the 5. leichte-Division (later the 21. Panzer-Division) was sunk en route to Africa and only dressings and first-aid items could be brought in by air. It was only following the arrival of the 15. Panzer-Division that a complete dressing station with ambulances and a field hospital was available. The 90. leichte-Division would arrive later, itself lacking any medical unit at all. During the Tobruk siege, Italians also had to be provided with medical assistance. Shuffling available units amongst the division could provide only an ad hoc, and at times inadequate, solution.

The overall situation would improve in early 1942, thanks largely to acquired experience and an improved supply situation. Problems were still encountered concerning the evacuation of the sick and wounded to rear areas, and from there to Europe, owing to British interdiction of the German supply lines. Once brought back to Tripoli, these soldiers would take the same route as the replacements, but going in the opposite direction; they would be embarked in a transport plane that took them to Italy (Greece later in the year), and from there back to Germany. One of the (often overlooked) strains imposed on the soldiers of the Afrikakorps was the lack of leaves of absence; this was quite a heavy burden given the fact that, even during lull or rest periods, there were hardly any distractions available. Leave was granted only

A PzKpfw III at a dressing station (*Hauptverbandplatz*, or *HVPL* as shown by the sign), probably after one of its crew has been wounded in combat. The tank's dark-grey colour and the pith helmet suggest that this photograph was taken early in 1941. (Carlo Pecchi collection)

at the end of June 1941, and even then it was very limited; only two soldiers per unit (generally a company) were granted a leave of three weeks (a longer period than average, because of desert service) after four months of service in North Africa, which was calculated as starting from the day after they sailed from Italy. This state of affairs did not last for long, and soon leave was prohibited because of the situation at the front. In the 21. Panzer-Division periods of leave were granted again on 20 September 1942, after prohibition had been enforced on 20 May, but only those who had served for more than a year in North Africa were granted a period of leave back to Germany. Limited transport facilities were available, so personnel were brought back by air with the sick and the wounded being granted priority. This heavily curtailed the number of those who could actually spend their leave as intended.

Drinkable water was another major issue in North Africa; washing was permitted using non-drinkable water only, which was itself scarce and all too often it was salty sea water. During battle or combat operations it was strictly prohibited to wash at all, which resulted in a great number of vermin, and

A convoy moving along the Via Balbia to the front; built in the 1930s and named after the governor of Libya, Italo Balbo, this was the only paved road in the area and stretched along the coast. It often (as is the case here) zigzagged in mountainous areas such as the 'Green Mountains' in Cyrenaica. (HITM)

 BRINGING THE WOUNDED BACK HOME, 1942

Since early 1942 troops were transferred from the European mainland to North Africa by air, mostly aboard the Junkers Ju 52 transport plane. Flights followed routes carrying them to Greece and Crete and from there to Libya or Egypt. A peak was reached in summer 1942, when a large number of new troops were hurriedly transferred to the Alamein line to face the crisis on the battlefield. Heavy weapons, vehicles and supplies were brought in by ships. On their way back home the transport planes would carry the wounded or sick, but also (to a limited extent) soldiers that had been granted a period of leave back to Germany. Since the Ju 52 carried only 18 men there were not many of these flights. On paper, soldiers brought back to Europe had to be issued with a new set of desert clothing, but that was not always possible. The mixture of clothing worn by the wounded Afrikakorps soldiers seen here reflects the actual conditions; every soldier would adapt his clothing to be as comfortable as possible, which was a necessity given the environment. Some wore the jacket without the shirt, others the shirts only. The comparison that can be made here with the desert uniforms worn by Luftwaffe personnel is revealing; the latter were supplied with uniforms that were more comfortable and of better quality. Their jackets could be fastened at the collar, while the trousers were loose fitting with baggy legs and a practical pocket on the left thigh. The use of items from the European uniform, like the blue-grey *Feldmütze*, was relatively common.

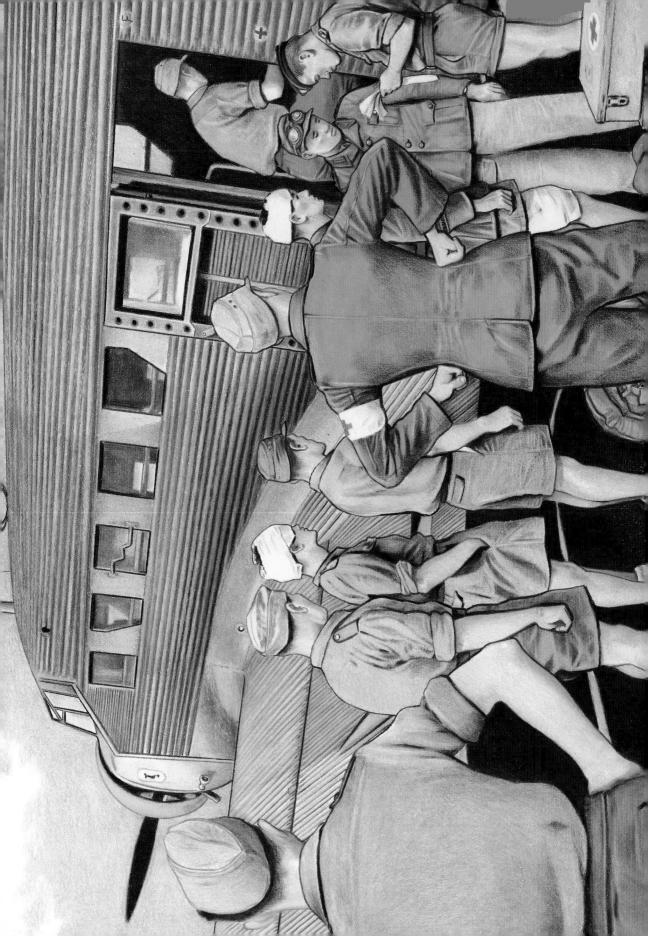

caused uniforms and underwear to suffer accordingly. Only cooking was relatively unaffected by the situation, since experiments resulted in bread eventually being made using sea water with positive results. It also seems that there were never serious shortages of drinkable water, even though some scarcity was experienced. During combat operations the daily ration issued was four to five litres per man, but in reality it was actually closer to three litres. This was, however, only issued to the field kitchens for cooking and for making tea and coffee. Individual soldiers would get a daily ration of three quarters of a litre, in the form of either water, tea or coffee, enough to fill their own canteen and intended to last for the entire day. This explains why some took care to acquire an extra canteen. There was never a proper solution found to the problem of keeping water cool in the desert.

BELIEF AND BELONGING

A PzKpfw II tank crew enjoys a moment of rest along with other Afrikakorps soldiers at a late stage of the campaign. Again, the mixture of uniforms is remarkable; the tank crew are wearing European denim fatigue uniforms (not intended for use in North Africa), one is wearing an overcoat and the uniforms of the other soldiers show different degrees of bleaching. (HITM)

The Afrikakorps is a name that eventually became a legend, owing to both its own reputation and that of its commander. In the whole of the German Army of World War II this is a unique case; there were other large formations led by famous and esteemed commanders (Guderian for example) but their renown never rose to anything like that of the Afrikakorps. Units could belong to these formations, but eventually they were switched to different commands and all that was left was the unit (a division, regiment or battalion) itself. Moreover, those soldiers seldom had any reason to feel somehow 'special', as their Afrikakorps comrades did; serving in France in 1940 or on the Eastern Front in 1941–43 was something completely different to serving in North Africa. Other soldiers shared your own experiences and sensations, the same daily

The crew of a PzKpfw III medium tank having a rest outside their vehicle. Worth noting are the heavily sun-bleached uniforms (indicating their status as veterans) and the large number of canteens carried on the back of the tank turret. The tank is painted in European dark grey, with an overspray of sand colour. (HITM)

life and the same enemy, but there were just too many of these soldiers, and the area too vast to make you feel like part of something extraordinary, distinct from the rest of the army. But that is exactly what the soldiers of the Afrikakorps would experience: they felt part of something different, something somehow special that they could share only amongst themselves – a relatively small group that was fighting a unique war in a unique theatre. It was the uniqueness of their situation that led to a feeling of distinction.

When they arrived in North Africa, the men of both the 5. leichte-Division and the 15. Panzer-Division had little in common; they fought in the same campaigns, but they did not share the same experiences (most of the former came from a Panzer division, and most of the latter from a reorganized infantry division). They also came from different areas of Germany. They were a hotchpotch of units, hurriedly sent to try and save a crumbling situation, yet it was this that would contribute to their forming their strong sense of belonging. In the spring of 1941 Germany was at war against Great Britain, a war that so far had been fought only by the men of the Luftwaffe or the Kriegsmarine. When they arrived in North Africa the men of the Afrikakorps knew they were the only soldiers in the German Army facing British forces on the battlefield, and that they were the vanguard of the German offensive against the British positions in the Middle East. This was a feeling strengthened by Rommel's belief, reiterated many times during the first advance into Cyrenaica, that their aim was to march into Egypt and seize the Suez Canal. With the beginning of Operation *Barbarossa*, the attack against the Soviet Union, the soldiers of the Afrikakorps might have known that theirs was no

A Focke Wulf 189 reconnaissance aircraft. Aerial observation was essential in the desert since it enabled one to discover where the enemy forces were and track their movements. The downside was that all too often it was hard to distinguish between friend and foe because of the dust clouds raised by the moving columns. (HITM)

longer Germany's main theatre of operations. It might not have been merely by chance that the 'Afrikakorps' cuff title was introduced shortly thereafter, in order to further strengthen their sense of belonging. Despite the increased focus on the Soviet Union, the men of the Afrikakorps still firmly believed that theirs was a vital strategic goal: to reach the Suez Canal and deliver Britain a staggering blow. In any case, their war was certainly not a sideshow.

One other thing that contributed to a large extent to the Afrikakorps soldiers' sense of belief and belonging was the fact that they were fighting in a harsh climate, which nobody else was experiencing. This added to the feeling of a sense of uniqueness. Also, they knew and they could see that all of them, regardless of rank and position, were going through the same appalling experiences. Frederick von Mellenthin, who served on Rommel's staff as intelligence officer, saw that Rommel would insist that he and the members of his staff be served the same food and rations as the troops. In Mellenthin's words: 'In North Africa this was not always a suitable diet; for months we had no fresh vegetables and lived only on tinned stuff; moreover the water was always brackish even in coffee or tea.' The most natural consequence of this was the spreading of illness and sickness not only amongst front-line soldiers, but also amongst those who served in the rear areas and in headquarters and staffs. Mellenthin again: 'We had many casualties from what the English call "gyppo tummy" and I myself had to leave North Africa in September 1942 with amoebic dysentery.' This was by no means an untypical experience.

Between spring 1941 and autumn 1942 a large number of Afrikakorps officers fell victim either to enemy fire or to sicknesses related to both climate and diet. Rommel went on sick leave twice, in March and from September to

October 1942, and his chief of staff Alfred Gause was wounded in June 1942 during the battle for the Gazala Line, along with Siegfried Westphal, with both men returning only in August. Ludwig Crüwell, who succeeded Rommel, was captured on 29 May 1942, and his own successor Walther Nehring was wounded on 31 August; Wilhelm von Thoma, who took over in September 1942, was captured on 4 November 1942 and two of his successors, Gustav Fehn and Kurt von Liebenstein, were both wounded. Five of the commanders of the 15. Panzer-Division suffered from a similar fate; Heinrich von Prittwitz und Gaffron, killed at Tobruk on 10 April 1941, was the first German general to fall victim to enemy fire in North Africa. His successor Hans-Karl von Esebeck was wounded on 25 July along with the man who replaced him, Walter Neumann-Silkow (wounded 6 December 1941). Gustav von Vaerst, who took over in December 1941, was wounded on 26 May 1942. After returning to the division in July, and after a brief spell as temporary commander of the Afrikakorps in September, he eventually fell victim to illness in November 1942. Johann von Ravenstein, the 21. Panzer-Division's commander, was captured on 29 November 1941; Georg von Bismarck, who took over in January 1942, was first wounded in July and eventually killed on 31 August (Heinz von Randow, who took over in September, was killed himself near Tripoli on 21 December 1942). The same fate was suffered by one of the 90. leichte-Division's commanders (Max Sümmermann, killed 10 December 1941), while another (Ulrich Kleemann) was wounded in September.

Command and leadership certainly played a vital role in the history of the Afrikakorps, and the best example is that of its legendary commander, Erwin Rommel. Even though he was a corps (and later army) commander his style of command (shaped by the 'lead from the front' concept common throughout the German Army) led him to be often at the front-line, with his troops. This could be quite a nightmare for his staff, and as Mellenthin put it quite clearly, his particular style of command did not always work well,

Enjoying a break at a command post in the desert. German headquarters were arranged in this way, with the lorries and buses spread out (a security measure in case of air attacks) and protected against the sun by tarpaulins. In 1941 even a fan was a luxury. (HITM)

with the result that 'decisions affecting the army as a whole were sometimes influenced unduly by purely local successes or failures'. A stern commander, Rommel 'could become most outspoken and very offensive to commanders of troops if he did not approve of their measures', a likely occurrence considering his habit of arriving at his headquarters at around 0500hrs, studying the situation reports and then heading out for an inspection of the front (where the whole day would be spent) accompanied by a staff officer. Such a style of command, although not without ill effects, would soon give Rommel a high status amongst the men of the Afrikakorps, making him extremely popular amongst his soldiers and setting an example they would follow. His vitality, along with his spartan habits (such as eating enlisted men's rations), led to his frequent inspections and his attention to details being seen by the troops not as an unnecessary intrusion, but rather as a sign of his care for them. Thus, while he could be a nightmare for officers, he was also 'very popular with young soldiers and NCOs, with whom he cracked many a joke' according to Mellenthin. As Luck pointed out: 'Everyone there spoke only of "Rommel", not of the General, so popular was he with his men; he was one of them'. This is clearly described by Otto Henning, whose unit was visited once by Rommel in May 1942; he arrived in his Storch (reconnaissance plane) in full uniform, with the officers' peaked cap sporting the famous goggles, and black boots. This detail caught Henning's attention, who wondered whether generals got sweaty feet too. Although rather uneventful, the incident made a strong impression upon the young soldier; Rommel left soon after, after a talk with the unit commander, and, before

A captured Daimler 'Dingo' armoured car, pressed into German service and turned into a communications vehicle, during a temporary halt in an Arab camp. Also note the MG 34 gun barrel protruding from the inside. (HITM)

boarding the plane, while it was being started, he just stood there with the soldiers two or three metres away, as if he were one of them. He was a legendary general, and yet one who could interact closely with his men.

Naturally, there was a downside; the strict discipline of the German Army suffered heavily from the slackened attitude developed by Afrikakorps soldiers as a result of the harsh environment, the climate and Rommel's style of command. This was emphasized by dress, which (also owing to its inadequacy) strayed further and further from regulations and often became heavily personalized, and also by the informal atmosphere between men of different ranks. Orders were issued on these matters, strictly asking to keep and maintain discipline and regulations, though this did not affect the general attitude, which was still somehow relaxed. One clothing-related accident is revealing of the sense of belonging within the Afrikakorps. Until early 1942 it had been rather a small group, lacking a large number of new intakes, which had the effect of further strengthening the ties between the men, who were hardened both to battle and to the desert. It was only since early 1942 that a large number of new replacements (often recruits) started to arrive in North Africa, mixing with the old veterans, known as the '*alte Afrikaner*' (old Africans). The latter would notice something strange: replacements' field caps would bleach unusually quickly. The trick soon became clear: they had learnt to wash their caps in water with the addition of some tablets of Losantin (used to protect against chemical warfare), which made them discolour very rapidly. Everybody wanted to look like the '*alte Afrikaner*', and everybody wanted to feel that sense of belonging to a renowned elite.

On parade, ready for inspection. Discipline amongst the Afrikakorps tended to slacken with time, which required attention from a senior level, and even from Rommel himself. (HITM)

This was a feeling more common amongst front-line troops, though they would all feel somewhat 'special' simply because they were serving in a unique environment.

This camaraderie did not last long, however; heavy losses, stress and fatigue soon took their toll, even amongst the '*alte Afrikaner*'. In July 1942, near El Alamein, a *Kampfgruppe* of the 90. leichte-Division ran into British defences and came under intense artillery fire; this was not a new experience, but this time they had just taken too much of it. Panic spread, and the officers had only one solution: to have the men leave their vehicles and entrench in order to create cover. The group was under fire for two days, suffering minimal losses amongst men but losing all their vehicles to artillery fire. The panic was eventually subdued, and the unit was even able to beat off an enemy tank attack, but the lorries could not be recovered. The war in the desert had a new direction: entrenchment, defences and positional warfare were now commonplace. This was not something the Afrikakorps had been used to, and yet something the replacements and the new units were keener to experience than fighting in the open. The spirit of the old Afrikakorps began to fade, and a few months later, in Tunisia, the few '*alte Afrikaner*' left would experience something unusual: one of their tanks, facing a determined enemy, withdrew. They could not help but comment that nothing like that would ever have happened in the old Afrikakorps.

EXPERIENCE OF BATTLE

The Afrikakorps' first drive into Cyrenaica in April 1941 was exhilarating, but it was only against the defences of Tobruk that the German soldiers would experience their real taste of battle in North Africa. After some initial attacks, on 30 April a new offensive was launched in the area of Ras el Mdauuar. The result was a near disaster, and resulted in some appalling experiences. After a march of 1,500km, of which 600km were across the desert, the German units were tired, and in some cases (such as within the motorcycle battalion) still dealing with unsuitable equipment. Rommel gave his first verbal orders to attack on 25 April, only to face criticism and

MACHINE-GUN POSITION, EL ALAMEIN, OCTOBER 1942
The most effective defence position in the desert was the simple dugout – a pit in the ground protected at the front by some rocks. The advantage was that it was hard to see, and even more hidden when it was covered with tarpaulins or wood and sand. The disadvantage was it was cramped and uncomfortable to live in. This machine-gun position (note the MG 34 with bipod) includes the usual crew of three. The variety of uniforms is typical of this stage of the war in North Africa, and it was not unusual for some soldiers to wear an overcoat while others stood in shirtsleeves. The soldier on the left, an *Obergefreiter* (private first class) has the new model of jacket (worn without the shirt) introduced in 1942, which lacked centre pleats on the pockets. The man in the centre, in shirtsleeve order, wears the new model of shirt, which lacked supports for shoulder straps. The shorts, otherwise much appreciated in rear areas or during rest time, proved quite unsuitable in the field as they were cut too high and offered no protection at all to the knees. When possible, Italian or British ones were used instead. The overcoat worn by the soldier on the right is the brown-olive-coloured one purpose-made for the desert, cut in the same style as the *Feldgrau* European one, with later models adopting the wide collar as well. Weapons include a Karabiner 98K rifle and an MP 40 submachine gun.

A 37mm Pak 35/36 gun emplacement somewhere in the Western Desert, 1941. The gun crew is unshaven, because during combat an order not to shave was issued in order to conserve water. The case in the foreground is for gun ammunition. (HITM)

uneasiness about the plan. Despite the fact that some units of the 15. Panzer-Division were still en route to North Africa, Rommel would not agree to a postponement; moreover, he forbade the commanders, for security reasons, from reconnoitring the area of the attack. It was only thanks to a previous reconnaissance carried out on 27 April that Kampfgruppe Kirchheim was spared greater losses.

The German air attack against the British positions started as scheduled at 1815hrs on 30 April, and half an hour later the advance parties of 5. leichte-Division's Maschinengewehr-Bataillon 2 and of the accompanying 2nd company of Pionier-Bataillon 39 moved forward, closing up to the barbed-wire defence without any opposition from the enemy. Immediately afterwards, at 1900hrs, the German artillery opened fire, while the Pionier parties were working on the wire, opening gaps through which the infantry could move forward to attack. Nobody realized what had happened: assault parties shifted west of the intended breakthrough positions, and the fact was neither noticed nor reported. Once gaps were opened a self-propelled 20mm gun moved past the wire, hitting a mine that set it ablaze; this lit up the area and attracted enemy fire, including mortars. Engineer and machine-gun companies moved forward to attack the enemy strongpoint, but bumped into one another in the dark and were not able to attack. Links with unit commanders were lost, and it was only thanks to the efforts of the commander of Maschinengewehr-Bataillon 2, Major Voigtsberger, that troops were gathered together and brought close to the target.

The morning after, owing to the approaching Panzers, Australian troops left their positions in the target area, which were seized by the Germans. This brought an unpleasant revelation; the open-topped 'Tobruk' bunkers, built to stand only a few feet above the ground, could not be easily spotted and they had also effectively protected the enemy soldiers from the effects of the air and ground bombardments. The Germans succeeded in advancing past the outer ring of the Tobruk defences, only to find themselves in open ground and under heavy artillery fire. Lack of experience and inadequate training were amongst the causes of units losing orientation, which resulted in their moving away from their targets, unable to find them in the dark. Eventually, the 5. leichte-Division alone lost 40 men killed in action, 122 wounded

Combined-arms warfare: a PzKpfw III medium tank halts close to an SdKfz 251/1 half-tracked troop transport laden with *Schützen*, or *Panzergrenadiere* as they were called from July 1942. (HITM)

and 45 missing. The total within the 15. Panzer-Division was heavier with 75 killed, 237 wounded and 83 missing. It would take intensive training and reorganization before the Afrikakorps could effectively assault the Tobruk defences.

In June 1941 the German soldiers started to experience how intense the desert heat could be. The men of the 15. Panzer-Division's Aufklärungs-Abteilung 33 deployed in the Sollum area started to experience how stressful it could be when the temperature was 40°C in the shade, and worse on a hot

A PzKpfw III tank negotiating a sand dune. Note the large number of grenades attached to the turret, probably intended for close defence. (HITM)

day. Heat and dust affected men, weapons and vehicles alike but did not hamper their effectiveness; units of the reconnaissance detachment carried out their security patrols and their reconnaissance behind enemy lines as usual. After 10–11 June the British became more and more active, both with their own patrols and with intensive air activity. On 11 June there was an air attack by British Hurricanes against 2. Kompanie during the mid-afternoon roll-call by the field kitchen; machine-gun fire killed two men and wounded four. Four days later the British attack (Operation *Battleaxe*) began. While the German guns (mainly 88mm anti-aircraft guns) defended the positions at Capuzzo and Sollum, the reconnaissance detachment deployed later in the morning in the area of Sidi Azeiz, ready to move forward against the enemy. Suddenly a group of a dozen British armoured cars attacked it, firing at the soft-skinned vehicles that withdrew to the west. The German armoured cars, supported by self-propelled 47mm guns on Panzer I carriages, held the enemy back and moved 2km north, where they regrouped and redeployed in 'hedgehog' defence, with anti-tank weapons in the outer positions and soft-skinned vehicles inward. The British armoured cars did not attack and the detachment resumed its reconnaissance duties.

A platoon moved forward to Maddalena and the enemy was sighted 300m from it; the Germans took up their defensive positions and did not reveal themselves. Instead, they started to follow the enemy vehicles, though they were soon forced to give this up because the enemy's numbers were too great, and they began to be fired upon. They decided to try again, and moved east toward their objective. Once more they faced enemy fire, an armoured car was hit but without sustaining damage, and this time the platoon reached Maddalena. Here a British tank column was spotted, composed of the dreaded Matilda tanks. The news was reported at once, and a few moments later their platoon was spotted and the British armour started their attack. In order to avoid enemy fire, the German armoured cars withdrew west, eventually reaching the Via Balbia in the area of Capuzzo, later to rejoin their unit.

The 'winter battle' (or Operation *Crusader* as it was known to the British) was the first major combat action the Afrikakorps faced during the campaign in the Western Desert. One of the most distinctive battles was the one fought on 23 November 1941, the 'Sunday of the dead'. The 15. Panzer-Division's Schützen-Regiment 200, along with the attached Pionier-Bataillon 33 and a company from the divisional anti-tank detachment, was regrouping in the Bir

 BRINGING FORWARD THE ANTI-TANK GUNS, GAZALA, MAY 1942

The much dreaded '88' anti-aircraft and anti-tank gun eventually became a synonym for German anti-tank guns in general, even though it was never available in large quantities and most actual kills were achieved by other guns like the 50mm Pak 38 or the 76.2mm Pak 36. The Flak 36/37 or 41 88mm gun was in use only with the Luftwaffe's *Flak Abteilung*, or anti-aircraft detachment, which was equivalent to a battalion. The army counterpart at the time was the *Flieger Abwehr Abteilung* that, missing the '*Kanone*' word from the *Flieger Abwehr* acronym, was equipped only with light 20mm guns. The first to arrive in North Africa was I Abteilung of Flak-Regiment 33, followed by I Abteilung of Flak-Regiment 18, which later formed the core of Flak-Regiment 135. This, along with Flak-Regiment 102, eventually formed the 19. Flak-Division attached to the Afrikakorps. As shown here, the typical German tactic envisaged close cooperation between infantry and anti-tank guns; in this case the '88' has been brought forwards, close to the infantry positions (intended to protect it), to get closer to the British tanks and destroy them before they can overrun the infantry. How successful this tactic was is demonstrated by the fact that, during the Sollum battle of June 1941, the guns of I/Flak-Regiment 33 alone destroyed some 80 British tanks.

The forward command post of the Afrikakorps' headquarters, probably during the 'winter battle' of November–December 1941 (also known as Operation *Crusader*). In the foreground is an SdKfz 251/3 radio command half-track, and in the background is one of the captured British AEC Matador command vehicles that were renamed 'Mammoths' by the Germans.

el Gubi area when, at 1300hrs, orders were received to attack the strong enemy forces deployed to the north along with Panzer-Regiment 5, with the aim of destroying them. The plan called for a Panzer spearhead, with mechanized infantry following up aboard vehicles. When the attack started at 1430hrs problems started to arise. Not having had enough time to prepare, the infantry lost contact with the Panzers and when the enemy positions were approached it was clear that the Panzers had taken another route; the infantry was alone. Thinking on his feet, the commander of Maschinengewehr-Bataillon 2, Major Debschütz, decided to dismount his men and deploy the companies' heavy weapons in position for a march attack; in spite of the lack of any support, artillery in particular, Debschütz took the lead and with his men stormed the positions of an enemy artillery regiment. Two batteries were overrun, many prisoners were taken and a mixed group of German anti-aircraft and anti-tank guns had in the meantime intervened on his right flank, fighting off an enemy armoured counter-attack. At about 1610hrs contact was established with the rest of the regiment and, less than one hour later, it was on the march again in order to attack a large concentration of enemy forces 1.5km away; this was poorly timed, since the enemy was ready and determined to meet them. The German soldiers approached the enemy positions under heavy fire, eventually deploying 200m away from them. With the heavy weapons once more in position, at dusk the infantry regrouped and started its attack. Soon, the enemy was in rout, leaving behind many prisoners, the wounded and the corpses of the dead. Soon it was all over, the night was uneventful and contact was established with the other German units the morning after. The German casualties were not heavy with ten men killed, 46 wounded and 61 missing; all in all some 600 enemy prisoners were taken.

During the spring of 1942 the Afrikakorps soldiers refined their skills, taking advantage of experience gained. In May they were ready to attack again, and the veterans knew that this would not be easy; the enemy was ready, the Gazala defence line was well prepared and the balance of forces again favoured the British. They were determined to succeed however. Tobruk was their next objective, and from there Egypt and the Suez Canal could be taken. During the night of 26–27 May the 21. and 15. Panzer-Divisionen regrouped west of Gazala ready to outflank the defence line and storm the enemy from the rear. They started moving in the dark at 2100hrs, covering some 50km in seven hours. At about 0300hrs on 27 May they reached the intended rest area south of Bir Hacheim, where vehicles were refuelled and the men took the chance to snatch a little sleep. Just before dawn the columns set off again. The divisional spearhead was I. Bataillon, Panzer-Regiment 5 of the 21. Panzer-Division, along with the *Panzerjäger* (anti-tank) detachment to its right. The men woke at 0330hrs, and one hour later the march began, in close order. The battalion adopted the classical wedge-shape deployment, with two companies in the lead and three in the rear, along with the battalion headquarters; all in all, the formation included 80 Panzers, including light and medium types. Very soon the British artillery began to fire on them, but they continued to press forwards.

Nine Panzer IIIs and three Panzer IIs had to withdraw because of mines, and the entire sixth company fell out of formation and became easy prey for the enemy artillery. As they were trying to rescue the damaged tanks, enemy artillery shells started to fall amongst them together with machine-gun and anti-tank fire. This was countered by the machine guns from one of the tanks still rolling, while tanks were recovered. Soon the company was on the move again, and eventually it rejoined the rest of the battalion in late afternoon, under constant enemy fire. This was from aircraft at first, then from artillery, and finally came the British armoured counter-attack. At dusk the battalion and indeed the entire division was now well behind enemy lines, to the north-east of Bir Hacheim. With the onset of darkness, confusion reigned; unable to make out friend from foe, some started to fire at will, sometimes hitting their own comrades. All of a sudden, a radio message was received: enemy

A forward headquarters position in the desert, showing how the vehicles were dispersed as a preventive measure against enemy artillery fire and air attacks. On the left is a Phänomen Granit ambulance close to a Kübelwagen, both sporting the red cross. On the right is an SdKfz 250/3 command half-track and in the background a mixture of armoured cars and staff cars can be seen. (US National Archives)

A Luftwaffe column on the move, probably belonging to a *Flak Abteilung*, one of the anti-aircraft detachments attached to the Afrikakorps. Note in the background a British Humber truck, one of the many vehicles captured and pressed into Afrikakorps service. (HITM)

infantry were infiltrating into the gaps between two companies. Flares of every kind and colour lit the sky, and Italian flame-thrower tanks approached and started to fire against the enemy. Then there was calm. At about 0300hrs on 28 May the tank crews took some rest, got out of their vehicles to eat something and stretch. It had all started 24 hours before, and the battle was still just beginning.

The decisive battle for Tobruk lasted for three weeks, but the prize was eventually won. Rommel took his chance and ordered to advance into Egypt, and the Afrikakorps followed him. In ten days they advanced deep into Egypt, seized Mersa Matruh and reached the El Alamein line; it was a time of excitement and exhilaration. Never before had the Nile seemed so close, and it never would be again. On 1 July 1942 Otto Henning was serving as a dispatch rider with his unit, Aufklärungs-Abteilung 580 of the 90. leichte-Division. It had had a hard time at the Alamein defence box; the enemy was not giving up. On 3 July a new attack was started, and Henning's company moved forward but again the enemy raked it with relentless fire and air attacks and the advance was halted. Bad news soon came; the New Zealanders had overrun Italian troops on the flank of the 90. leichte-Division. A counter-attack was arranged and Henning set out along with his unit. Soon they came under artillery fire again, and Henning could not help closing in with his *Kübelwagen* to his commander's vehicle, which made him feel safer. The unit deployed, ready to face enemy armour, and soon enough the attack came, together with heavy artillery fire. Henning, who spoke a little Italian, was sent back to seek medical help, but he did not manage to find any. He rushed back to his unit and, under heavy artillery fire again, he ran into what was left of the vehicle of the unit commander. It had been hit. Henning's commander, Hauptmann Friedrich von Homeyer, was dead, and another officer was wounded. He would die later the same day. Henning was shocked; Homeyer had shaped him into a

soldier, and he knew that he could always rely on him. But there was no time to grieve, as the following day the division gave up its attack and took up defensive positions to the south of El Alamein. On the night of 5–6 July the New Zealanders attacked again, breaking through their positions. It was the beginning of a long battle, which would eventually end four months later with the ultimate defeat and withdrawal of the Afrikakorps. For the Afrikakorps soldiers there was no longer any feeling of excitement or exhilaration, only the determination to fight.

The 88mm Flak 36/37 or 41 dual-purpose anti-aircraft and anti-tank gun being serviced during a lull in the fighting. Manned by Luftwaffe personnel, it was the most effective anti-tank weapon in the Afrikakorps' inventory. (HITM)

A *Kübelwagen* along with two radio armoured cars of the kind that saw widespread use amongst the Panzer divisions. To the left is the small four-wheeled SdKfz 223 and to the right the large eight-wheeled SdKfz 263. (HITM)

AFTER THE BATTLE

The last battle of El Alamein started on 23 October 1942, and some two weeks later the Axis forces were defeated, in large part destroyed, and what was left of them began a long withdrawal. The Afrikakorps had fought its last major battle in the Western Desert, and for the next seven months it would be back on the offensive only briefly, and not against its long-time enemy, the British Eighth Army. But this was no longer the old Afrikakorps, the one that had fought and won the battles of 1941–42. In late November 1942 Rommel reported that its combat strength was down to the size of a reinforced regiment, even though its total strength still stood at about 40,000 men. Losses had been high, simply too high for an already worn-out combat unit that had sustained heavy suffering amongst its fighting troops. The Afrikakorps was now just an empty shell; its combat strength would be somewhat restored in February 1943, but nothing approaching the level it had been at previously. The Tunisian campaign was merely a last act, and was no longer a campaign to try and win a decisive victory in North Africa. New men were taken in, and the old ones kept fighting for some more months before the final surrender. Eventually, the final surrender of 13 May 1943 put an end to the Axis presence in North Africa. Alamein had cost the Afrikakorps and the Axis troops something in the region of around 40,000 prisoners and 20,000 killed and wounded. Tunisia would add another 270,000-odd German and Italian soldiers to the list, with the total toll for the North African campaign standing for the Axis forces at about 620,000 men (there are no detailed figures for specifically German losses).

Tent quarters in the desert, probably near an airport as suggested by the propeller on the ground. It is interesting to note that the camouflaged shelter quarters (or *Zeltbahn*) intended for use in Europe also saw widespread use in the desert, even though the camouflage was completely useless. (HITM)

On 23 February 1943 Rommel relinquished command of Panzerarmee Afrika to the Italian Generale Messe. The army was renamed as the First Italian Army, with a mixed German and Italian staff. On 9 March he would leave North Africa for the last time, never to return to his Afrikakorps. It fought the last battles until the surrender in May against its old enemy, the British Eighth Army, and thereafter the Afrikakorps ceased to exist. The 15. Panzer-Division and the 90. leichte-Division were restored to life as the 15. and 90. Panzergrenadier Divisionen, both of which went on to distinguish themselves in the Italian campaign. There were hardly any Afrikakorps veterans in them, formed as they were from Afrikakorps replacement units bound for the Tunisian battlefield who never made it. In France the 21. Panzer-Division was rebuilt again, later to distinguish itself in Normandy, but it bore little if any resemblance to the old one, divisional insignia apart (Afrikakorps veteran Hans von Luck commanded a *Panzergrenadier* unit made up of veterans from the Eastern Front). There were still Afrikakorps veterans in some German units, proudly sporting the 'Afrika' cuff title, but there was no longer an Afrikakorps. It was impossible that there could be.

Most of the Afrikakorps soldiers became prisoners of war. Those who were captured at El Alamein or earlier went into British hands, and those captured in Tunisia went in large part into American hands. Their recollections speak of experiences probably common to all POWs, or at least most of them. Those in American hands enjoyed decent food and were, generally speaking, not treated very badly. This was not always the case for

Towing an 88mm Flak 36/37 to its position, where it could fire at long range against British armour. The gun tractor is a Krauss Maffei SdKfz 7 half-track, a very sturdy and versatile unarmoured vehicle with excellent cross-country capabilities in the desert. (Carlo Pecchi collection)

those in British captivity, who suffered from a lack of food, hard work and an unconcealed acrimony from their captors. Prisoners were brought back to the European mainland, and were subsequently released in 1946–47. This happened only after a denazification process, which had POWs subdivided into three groups: Nazis, or those who had enthusiastically shown sympathy and support for Germany and the Nazi regime (or even just refused to cooperate); the 'nominal members' or *Mitläufer*, those who proved themselves quite unconcerned about political matters; and the anti-Nazis or those who opposed the Nazi regime. Needless to say the latter were the first to be sent back home. The other POWs had to wait, but their label did not always mean that they were exactly what they were supposed to be; at times even an uncooperative or reluctant attitude might be enough to lead to somebody being described as a Nazi or a *Mitläufer*. Most importantly, these POWs perceived the German defeat in quite a different way to those who had fought until the last. News was slow to reach them, and many knew that what they heard had been filtered through Allied propaganda, which made them somewhat sceptical. All in all the overriding feeling left in them was a sense of defeat, not a preoccupation with the collapse of Germany and of the Nazi regime. Return home must not have been a happy time, to find that everything had changed and to be confronted with the hardships that had been experienced by those who had remained.

What was left for both the ex-POWs and the other Afrikakorps veterans was a sense of belonging. Together they had lived through a unique experience, and fought and risked their lives in a harsh and unpleasant theatre of war under the command of one of the most respected German generals. They had been part of something, and it was a part of their lives that would not be forgotten. Soon after the end of the war, veterans' associations were formed, and those who had been part of the Afrikakorps joined together once more to remember their experiences and to help and support each other. In 1950 the first peacetime issues of the magazine *Die Oase* (*The Oasis*) would appear, already published in wartime as a kind of 'official' magazine for the Afrikakorps. It was now the official magazine of the Verband Deutsches Afrikakorps (DAK association) and of the Rommel Sozialwerk (Rommel's social work) veterans' organizations, which encompassed all Afrikakorps

H **THE AFRIKAKORPS' LAST STAND, TUNISIA, 1943**

Following the defeat at El Alamein and the creation of the Tunisian bridgehead in November 1942 the last phase of the war in North Africa began. By February 1943 the Afrikakorps, having retreated all the way from Alamein to the Tunisian border, met with the newly arrived forces in Tunisia. The contrast between the two was striking, as was reflected by the differences in uniform shown here. On the left a veteran *Unteroffizier* from the 21. Panzer-Division, armed with an MP 40 submachine gun, is wearing an old (1941) jacket with shorts. He wears the 'Afrikakorps' cuff title (**1**), officially discontinued after the introduction of the new 'Afrika' cuff title (**2**) on 15 January 1943, but still largely used by Afrikakorps veterans. The Afrikakorps palm and swastika insignia is shown at (**3**). The soldier on the right, from 10. Panzer-Division, is wearing a brand-new desert uniform (without pleat pockets), with a *Feldgrau* steel helmet and complete infantry webbing and equipment (which includes the assault pack with mess kit, blanket and camouflaged tent quarter), but in the leather version normally used with the European uniform. He is also wearing the standard low-cut boots with anklets, which had already been introduced for the Afrikakorps but had never proved to be very popular, in contrast to those who were sent to the Tunisian bridgehead. He is armed with a Karabiner 98K rifle. Three months after this meeting, in mid-May 1943, the last remnants of the German and Axis forces in Tunisia surrendered, putting an end to the campaign in North Africa.

2

1

3

veterans. War cemeteries and memorials were also built where the battles were fought to honour those who had died. Memorials shaped like Teutonic castles were built close to Tobruk and at El Alamein, the latter ringed by a memorial plate inscribed with the names of 4,200 dead German soldiers. In Tunisia a war cemetery was built on a hill near Hamman Lif. Every year thousands of tourists and travellers visit these memorials and war cemeteries, paying their tribute to the men who died in the war in North Africa, the men of the Afrikakorps.

Even though the Afrikakorps ceased to exist with the final surrender in Tunisia, its history had just begun. Both the name of this formidable fighting corps and of its legendary commander had earned notoriety and respect amongst their enemies. American General Omar Bradley considered them the best fighters he ever met during the war and described them as 'young men, early twenties, seasoned veterans… good physical condition. Never knew they were beaten'. According to some reports these men were still being captured in Tunisia as late as August 1943, when they eventually surrendered themselves after they had refused to give in until running completely out of food. After the war, the former enemies of the Afrikakorps would pay tribute by acknowledging the quality and the stature of those German soldiers they met and fought against during the campaign in North Africa. In the foreword to his *The Life and Death of the Afrikakorps*, Ronald Lewin wrote that: 'The Afrikakorps possessed not only the social characteristics of a family well

adapted to its environment, as well as a passionate sense of self-identity, but also that inner unity, that cohesion of part with part, which makes such a smooth-functioning organism not only biologically but also militarily efficient.' In other words, Afrikakorps soldiers were not just combatants, nor merely the components of a skilled, efficient armed unit. They were also (if not above all) men who, while fighting a war, had been able to work their way through a new, unfamiliar, harsh and hostile environment, itself as dangerous as their enemies were. They did it together all the way, supporting and helping each other. It was really a kind of family, a unique experience in the history of warfare and certainly in the lives of all of them.

When, on the night of 12–13 May 1943, the last commander of the Afrikakorps, General Hans Cramer, sent out the final message from the Afrikakorps before the final surrender, he took care to add a sentence that might sound unsuited to the moment. It was: 'The German Afrikakorps must rise again.' It did not do so as a combat unit, but it would rise again as an experience and as a history that united different generations, friends and enemies alike. I cannot think of a better way to conclude this work than to use the words that put an end to an epic campaign, and started a history still alive today: 'Ammunition shot off. Arms and equipment destroyed. In accordance with orders received Afrikakorps has fought itself to the condition where it can fight no more. The German Afrikakorps must rise again. Heia Safari!'

A heavy machine-gun position in the desert, probably in the El Alamein area in 1942. This position is typical: a simple dugout in the desert protected by a few stones. (HITM)

A Kübelwagen and Horch staff car get close to the remnants of a British armoured column in order to inspect the wreckage. In the background is a destroyed M3 Grant/Lee tank, and in the foreground a 2-pdr anti-tank gun can be seen on a portee. (HITM)

BIBLIOGRAPHY

Aberger, Heinz-Dietrich, *Die 5. (lei.)/21. Panzer Division in Nordafrika 1941–1943* (Preussischer Militär-Verlag: Reutlingen, 1994)

Battistelli, Pier Paolo, *Rommel's Afrika Korps: Tobruk to El Alamein* (Osprey: Oxford, 2006)

Behrendt, Hans-Otto, *Rommel's Intelligence in the Desert Campaign* (William Kimber: London, 1985)

Bender, Roger James and Law, Richard D., *Uniforms, Organization and History of the Afrika Korps* (R. J. Bender: Mountain View, 1973)

Boog, Horst, Rahn, Werner, Stumpf, Reinhard and Wegner, Bernd, *Das Deutsche Reich und der Zweite Weltkrieg* , Vol. 6 (DVA: Stuttgart, 1990)

Bradford, George R., *Rommel's Afrika Korps: El Agheila to El Alamein* (Stackpole: Mechanicsburg, PA, 2008)

Carell, Paul, *Die Wüstenfüchse: Mit Rommel in Afrika* (Nannen: Hamburg, 1958)

Forty, George. *Afrika Korps at War, Volume 1: The Road to Alexandria* and *Volume 2: The Long Road Back* (Ian Allan: London, 1978)

Fraser, David, *Knight's Cross: A Life of Field Marshal Erwin Rommel* (Harper Collins: New York, 1993)

Greene, Jack and Massignani, Alessandro, *Rommel's North African Campaign: September 1940–November 1942* (Combined Books: Conshohocken, PA, 1994)

Hahn, Fritz, *Waffen und Geheimwaffen des deutschen Heeres, 1933–1945* (Bernard & Graefe: Bonn, 1998)

Hartmann, Bernd, *Geschichte des Panzerregiments 5, 1935–1943, und der Panzerabteilung 5, 1943–1945* (private publication: Erftstadt, 2004)

Heckmann, Wolf, *Rommels Krieg in Afrika: Wüstenfüchse gegen Wüstenratten* (Gustav Lübbe: Bergisch Gladbach, 1976)

Henning, Otto, *Als Panzerschütze beim Deutschen Afrika Korps 1941–1943* (Flechsig: Würzburg, 2006)

Jackson, W. G. F., *The Battle for North Africa 1940–43* (Mason/Charter: New York, 1975)

Kitchen, Martin, *Rommel's Desert War: Waging World War II in North Africa, 1941–1943* (CUP: Cambridge, 2009)

Kriebel, Rainer, *Inside the Afrika Korps: The Crusader Battles, 1941–1942* (Stackpole: Mechanicsburg, PA, 2000)

Kühn, Volkmar, *Mit Rommel in der Wüste: Kampf und Untergang des Deutschen Afrika-Korps 1941–1943* (Flechsig: Würzburg, 2006)

Kurtz, Robert, *Afrika Korps: Tropical Uniforms, Insignia & Equipment of the German Soldiers in World War II* (Schiffer: Atglen, PA, 2004)

Latimer, Jon, *Tobruk 1941: Rommel's Opening Move* (Praeger: Westport, CT, 2004)

Lewin, Ronald, *The Life and Death of the Afrika Korps* (Pen & Sword: Barnsley, 2003)

Luck, Hans von, *Panzer Commander, The Memoirs of Colonel Hans von Luck* (Cassell: London, 1989)

Macksey, Kenneth, *Afrika Korps* (Ballantine: New York, 1968)

Mas, Cedric, *Afrika Korps*, 2 vols. (Batailles & Blindés: Aix-en-Provence, 2007–2008)

Mellenthin, F. W., *Panzer Battles: A Study of the Employment of Armour in the Second World War* (Futura: London, 1984)

Mitcham, Samuel W., *Rommel's Desert Commanders: The Men who Served the Desert Fox, North Africa, 1941–42* (Stackpole: Mechanicsburg, PA, 2007)

Mitcham, Samuel W., *Rommel's Desert War: The Life and Death of the Afrika Korps* (Stackpole: Mechanicsburg, PA, 2007)

Rolf, David, *The Bloody Road to Tunis: Destruction of the Axis Forces in North Africa, November 1942–May 1943* (Greenhill: London, 2001)

Rommel, Erwin, *The Rommel Papers* (Collins: London, 1953)

Schreiber, Gerhard, Stegemann, Bernd and Vogel, Detlef, *Das Deutsche Reich und der Zweite Weltkrieg*, Vol. 3 (DVA: Stuttgart, 1984)

Stolfi, R. H. S., *German Panzers on the Offensive: Russian Front – North Africa, 1941–1942* (Schiffer: Atglen, PA, 2003)

Taysen, Adalbert von, *Tobruk 1941: Der Kampf in Nordafrika* (Rombach: Freiburg, 1976)

Toppe, Alfred, *Desert Warfare: German Experiences in World War II* (US Army Command and General Staff College, 1991)

Watson, Bruce Allen, *Exit Rommel: The Tunisian Campaign, 1942–43* (Stackpole: Mechanicsburg, PA, 2007)

Williamson, Gordon, *Afrika Korps 1941–43* (Osprey: Oxford, 2001)

Windrow, Martin, *Rommel's Desert Army* (Osprey: Oxford, 1976)

www.deutsches-afrikakorps.de (contains several interviews with Afrikakorps veterans)

INDEX

Figures in **bold** refer to illustrations.